TIME to EAT

NADIYA HUSSAIN

TIME
TO
EAT

Delicious meals
for busy lives

PHOTOGRAPHY BY CHRIS TERRY

CLARKSON POTTER/PUBLISHERS
NEW YORK

DEDICATION

To the time-poor among us.
We rush, we scramble, and we get by.
In doing so, we live.
Rushed and frayed around the edges,
still we go on.
We smile. We frown. Unsteady yet firm.
"I have no time" we say in haste.

Don't we?

We have it, no matter how swift and
meaningless it feels.
We have it! We have time, it is ours!
However long or short, it is ours to take.

Let's rush, but sometimes let's just stop.
To Abdal, Musa, Dawud, and Maryam.

Originally published in hardcover in Great Britain by
Michael Joseph, a division of Penguin Random House
UK, London, in 2019. By arrangement with the BBC.

Library of Congress Cataloging-in-Publication Data
is available.

ISBN 978-0-593-23353-5
Ebook ISBN 978-0-593-23354-2

Printed in Canada

10 9 8 7 6 5 4 3

First American Edition

CONTENTS

HOW TO USE THIS BOOK
6

BREAKFAST
16

LUNCH
68

DINNER
126

DESSERTS
182

BASICS
234

INDEX
248

THANKS
254

HOW TO USE THIS BOOK

This book is unique and special because it introduces you to my world, my way of cooking, which can become your world and your way of cooking. It will help you become a time-smart cook without even really realizing it. I'm so excited to share all this with you. There are recipes that show you how to batch cook and how to use—and really appreciate—the space in your freezer. You can spin leftovers into whole new meals and make beautiful food that can be put together in very little time.

I don't want to appear condescending, I really don't. Or look like I know what I'm doing. But I kind of do! Not because I'm an expert, but because I know what it's like to have just one head and one pair of hands. We are all human. Cluttered minds, to-do lists that never seem to get smaller, stuff to do, and still only four limbs. We can only get to our destination as quickly as our legs can carry us. We can only prepare the family dinners that are needed with the two hands we have and whatever time is left at the end of the day. Yet life seems to treat us like we are octopuses, with eight limbs to juggle the laundry, the chores, wiping down surfaces, tying laces, shoveling in food, typing, swiping, clicking.

I haven't got it all figured out. I still don't know how to do the YMCA and knead bread at the same time. It's a work in progress, but I will do it! I'm not saying my way is the best way. But it's pretty good. This is the way I have been cooking for a decade and it really does work. All you need is a willingness to change how you cook a little, and to make a little freezer space. It's definitely not foolproof. It takes time and a little extra thinking, but ultimately when I cook like this, what happens is I get my cooking fill, I get to be creative and cook delicious food. I get to cook in advance. By spending just a little more time in the kitchen (and by little I mean not that much more), it means I'm cooking extra and freezing and saving for the week ahead. By the time I have done this for a few weeks, I find myself with a whole week free to do other things. Like have a bath, do some work knowing dinner is sorted, simply enjoy putting one foot in front of the other without worrying about the speed at which my feet are moving. Leaving me happy to be human and less envious of our eight-legged sea creature. I don't want to be the octopus, I want to cook him, eat him, freeze him, and enjoy him again the following week without breaking a sweat, without thinking.

This book has over 100 delicious recipes for you to choose from. Some take a little less time and others take a little more time, but there'll be a reason for it—you'll be creating a second meal to keep in the freezer, or you'll be using a component of the meal you are making to spin into something completely different tomorrow that won't require any preparation. Some are perfect for when you have no time to spare and others for when you have plenty of time. The difference with these recipes is that you have options. You can use frozen onions or fresh. You can use fresh veg or canned. You can make one recipe now and know that you have dinner in the freezer ready for the weeks ahead. You can make more sauce than you need for that dessert now and make a hot chocolate later.

In my first few weeks of cooking like this, I found I was busy cooking one week, cooking more than I needed, stocking my freezer and giving myself a week free of cooking, but safe in the knowledge that my family was eating home-cooked food. But after a few months I found I had food stocked up for weeks, so much so that I had to stop cooking for a while just to empty the freezer out. After six months, I was ready for every situation. Cake to take to a party? I had one in the freezer! Late home one night? It didn't matter because dinner just needed to be taken out and heated from frozen. Unexpected guests? I always had something to whip up fast. Late night? There was always something in the back of the fridge for when we got the munchies. If you want to test the theory, turn up at my home and I will have something for you—but I won't be slaving or panicking over a hot stovetop and a noisy oven.

I HAVE A FEW RULES
I ALWAYS TELL MYSELF

1

DON'T THROW
ANYTHING AWAY

As long as it's not poisonous,
you can probably do
something with it.

2

CANNED, FROZEN, AND DRY
ARE NOT BAD WORDS

They save time and money.
They keep for a long time
and save on waste.

3

THE FREEZER IS MY FRIEND

I always have one drawer totally
empty, having just that little bit
of space means you have room
to think on your feet.

4

EVERY DISH IS TWO DISHES

I always make a little bit more than
I need in the hope of turning one
meal into two, without having to
cook it twice.

5

EVERYTHING IS
AN INGREDIENT

You can make something
out of anything.

6

THE MICROWAVE CAN SAVE

It saves time and saves on the
gas bill. It's quick and really
very handy.

Throughout this book you will find lots of recipes where there appears to be just one recipe, but secretly there are two. It could be a double-up recipe or a recipe where you make a little more than you need, so you can make an entirely different dish as well. Don't be afraid if a recipe indicates it serves six if there are only two of you needing dinner tonight—you will most likely be able to freeze the leftovers, saving you cooking time later in the week. You'll find a short Basics section at the back of the book, too, which contains staple recipes you might like to make yourself, if you have time, though the main recipes will just as happily work with the store-bought version.

I can't promise everything, but what I can give you are delicious recipes that everyone can enjoy. What I can promise is a little insight into the way my mind works. This way of cooking has allowed me to free up time, and I reckon if you give it a go it can do the same for you. By the time you have gone through this book you will have mastered the art of cooking, eating, feeding, and doing it all over again, without actually doing it!

KEY

Each recipe shows an active time as well as a total time, where relevant, to show you where you can be saving even more time (for example, a 2-hour recipe that actually only requires 30 minutes of my time—before the oven does the rest of the work for me—means there's at least an hour to spend on other things).

You will also spot some ingredients listed in **bold**. These are where there are components of the recipe that can be doubled up or halved, and spun into a completely different dish. Just follow the instructions on each recipe. As you go through the book, you'll see the following symbols to help you plan your cooking time:

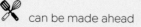 can be made ahead   ❄ recipe is freezable   🥫 double batch

USING YOUR FREEZER

My freezer is my absolute savior when it comes to preparing meals for my family. It took me a few years to work it out, but now I would not be without it. It not only means I can have stacks of meals in there, all ready to go, but I'll often have ingredients stashed away in there too, which saves any last-minute trips to the store when I've already whacked the oven on and the stove burners are going! So, when my husband asks me, "What do you want for your birthday?" before I can respond, he always says, "Don't say a freezer!" I would have another if I had the room, but I don't! So I make do with the one I have.

You'll see from many of the recipes in this book that I like to prepare a double batch so I can freeze half of it. I often do this on the weekend, when I have a little more time, and I'm always SO grateful for it when we're halfway through our busy weeks, trying to balance everyone's timetables and it feels like there's just no time left in the day for preparing a meal. If I can save on preparation time, it makes life so much easier in the long run. Plus, a full freezer is better for your energy bills—there is more cold air to circulate around a half-empty freezer, so keeping it nice and full is time AND energy efficient! And that is also pretty ace!

You might think from the number of dishes I freeze in this book that I have an industrial-size freezer! I don't, but I have learned along the way that it's all about how you organize it. I've included tips on how to do this in some recipes where there's an obvious hack (for example, I like to pour batter into a freezer-proof bag, which I then lay flat on a baking sheet and pop in the freezer so it freezes in a thin sheet—far easier to stack and store than clumpy Tupperware when you're short on space).

It sounds obvious, but always label whatever you're freezing with what it is and the date you made it. It might seem quicker to put things straight in the freezer rather than hunting around for a Sharpie, but it will make your life so much easier when you can see at a glance what you have in there. And although you always think you'll just remember what each dish is, I guarantee you will spend a considerable amount of time trying to work out what unlabeled frozen blocks of food are once a few weeks have gone by. Just don't do what I have done and try to write on an already frozen meal—moisture and ink don't like each other. Label first, fill second! I also always have a roll of wide masking tape in my kitchen drawers, for the Tupperware that I don't want permanent writing on. Stick it on, label and date it, and get it in the freezer. Then when you're done with it, peel it off and it's as good as new, ready for your next meal.

INGREDIENTS I OFTEN PREP AND FREEZE

I don't want to give you a definitive list of things you can and can't freeze, as this isn't intended to be a freezer manual. So much of it is learning as you go along, but if you find something you can freeze and I don't know about it, please tell me! Share with me on Instagram: @nadiyajhussain. We are all learning every day and I want to always be a part of that. You will find freezing instructions within each recipe, where it is relevant. But there are a few things I have learned that it's always handy to have a frozen stash of. It's always a huge relief when I want to make something but have a vital ingredient missing . . . then realize I have a bag of it in the freezer!

❄ GRATED CHEESE (4 months): I always have this in the freezer; just grate it straight into the ziplock bag it came in!

❄ CHOPPED ONIONS (8–10 months): Be sure to double-bag these. They are so handy to have when I'm rushed for time, but I don't want everything smelling of onions so I always double-bag.

❄ MOST FRUIT AND VEG (8–10 months) that might be going to waste in your fridge. (If I think I won't get around to using a broccoli, for example, I will cut it into florets and freeze in a freezer-proof bag.) Just not (raw) potatoes or salad.

❄ MILK (1 month): I don't often have milk in the freezer, but sometimes when we go away for the weekend, rather then frantically trying to use it all up I just pop it into the freezer and defrost in the fridge when I get back.

❄ BUTTER (12 months): Often when I need to freeze butter, I mix it with a clove of crushed garlic and then I have garlic butter on hand whenever I need it, be it on steak or just to rub onto naan. Even better on a baked potato!

❄ BREADCRUMBS (3 months): My breadcrumbs usually consist of the ends of a loaf of bread that nobody wants to eat.

❄ EGG WHITES (12 months): Freeze these labeled so you know how many you have in each bag, and you have egg whites for meringues whenever you want (for every egg white, you will need ¼ cup plus 1 tablespoon/60g sugar, added slowly to whipping egg whites and baked at 200°F/100°C for 1½ to 1¾ hours till they are crisp and dry).

❄ SPICE PASTES (3 months): Store in a ziplock bag or sealed in Tupperware.

❄ PESTO: As above.

❄ HERBS (12 months): This is really handy when you've bought a whole package but only need three sprigs for your recipe, and will save you from having to buy a whole new package the next time you need it! You can freeze these as they are in a ziplock bag or zap in the microwave for a few seconds till totally dry, then crush in the palm of your hand and collect in a jar.

❄ BREAD (3 months) and bread dough.

❄ CHILES (8–10 months): Again because you might not use the whole bag that you've bought. These can be grated straight into dishes from frozen.

TIPS FOR FREEZING

❄ MANY DISHES CAN BE COOKED FROM FROZEN, and these are indicated in the recipes. Remember that raw meat should always be fully defrosted before cooking.

❄ ALWAYS ALLOW FOOD TO COOL COMPLETELY BEFORE COVERING AND FREEZING. Putting anything that is still hot into the freezer will increase the overall temperature of your freezer . . . which may jeopardize all the other beautiful things you've already frozen.

❄ REMEMBER TO KEEP THE FREEZER SHUT IF THERE'S A POWER OUTAGE. Your food in there should be fine for twenty-four hours.

❄ MAKE SURE THINGS ARE WELL WRAPPED UP. I tend to use reusable silicone freezer bags, or I freeze things (such as lasagne, etc.) right in the dish I'd like to cook them in (just make sure it's suitable for the freezer). If using plastic wrap or aluminum foil, make sure it's really well wrapped and ideally pop in a resealable bag or a Tupperware container. This will keep your food free from freezer burn (although if you do find these little brown spots on frozen food, it's not harmful).

❄ I TEND TO FREEZE THINGS IN THE PORTION SIZES I KNOW I WILL NEED, which is often for all 5 of us. Try to do the same to avoid waste, as you don't want to be defrosting more than you can use.

❄ FOR SMALL ITEMS, such as falafel, freeze on a baking sheet and then pop in a freezer bag once frozen (this will prevent them from freezing into one big joined-up clump!). Or just freeze them in a clump and then slam it on the worktop to separate them—that's the fun way to do it!

❄ THE SAFEST WAY TO DEFROST FOOD IS FOR SEVERAL HOURS IN THE FRIDGE UNTIL FULLY THAWED. If you want to speed this process up slightly, you can place the freezer bag or container in a large bowl of cold or room temperature water.

❄ DON'T REFREEZE FOOD ONCE IT HAS THAWED unless it has been cooked thoroughly (e.g., if you defrost some ground meat to then make into a lasagne, which you cook, you can then freeze that cooked lasagne).

❄ IF YOU HAVE LEFTOVERS, BUT NOT ENOUGH TO FEED THE WHOLE FAMILY, I would invest in some small ovenproof single-portion containers and when you have enough for a solo meal, freeze it. When it's late at night and you don't fancy cooking, and all you want is that meal you had last week . . . you can have it.

❄ MY FREEZER HAS BEEN MY SAVIOR IN SO MANY WAYS. I want to be that ethical person, I want to do it all, and that's not always possible, but every time I save something from ending up in the trash or I reduce a tiny bit of waste, I feel better. Because really, I'm no superhero. All I want is to save money, save time, and feed my family—and when I don't waste in and among all of that, I feel a million times better.

BREAKFAST

Who says you can't have cheesecake for breakfast? Wrap it in a croissant and I reckon it's totally acceptable. These are so simple to make, and with lots of that filling left over, there's enough to make breakfast for another day as well, so I've suggested you make some Creamy Raspberry Overnight Oats. If you prefer not to make that at the moment, simply halve the quantities of the ingredients in **bold** to make your croissants.

RASPBERRY CHEESECAKE CROISSANTS

2 cups/500g ricotta (or soft full-fat cream cheese)

¼ cup/50g sugar (or vanilla sugar, if you have any)

2 teaspoons vanilla extract (optional)

2½ cups/300g fresh or frozen raspberries

2 tablespoons all-purpose flour

1 large egg

6 all-butter croissants

Preheat the oven to 400°F/200°C and have a 12-hole muffin pan at the ready. I know we are only making 6, but they just need a bit of room—plus I don't know many people who own a 6-hole muffin pan, I have never had one. I can't see the sense in making 6 muffins when you can make 12, but in this instance, it is perfect.

Whisk the ricotta in a bowl to loosen, then add the sugar and vanilla and mix really well. Add the raspberries and give them a stir, so that they don't break up too much, but bleed enough to give that lovely marbled effect.

If you are making the overnight oats as well, place half the mixture in a Tupperware container with a lid and set aside—see opposite for how to use this. Now add the flour and egg to the remaining mixture and mix really well.

Cut each croissant horizontally, the way you would cut them if you were going to butter and jam them but not all the way through. Open them up and fit them inside the holes of your muffin pan—you are aiming for what looks like a croissant shell cup. You might need to press lightly, to open the croissant. Do this to all 6 croissants, then fill with the ricotta mixture.

Bake in the oven for 15 minutes. There should be a gentle wobble in the center. These are delicious eaten straight away, but equally delicious chilled from the fridge if you have any left over. They will keep for 3 days in the fridge.

If you plan on freezing them, pop them into a freezer bag (if you have several, freeze them uncovered on a baking sheet for 1 hour first. Then pop into a freezer bag).

CREAMY RASPBERRY OVERNIGHT OATS

Having breakfast all ready for you in the morning is one of the greatest ways to save time. While the croissants are baking, add ½ cup plus 2 tablespoons/150ml of whole milk to the mixture in the Tupperware. Add 1⅔ cups/150g of uncooked rolled oats and mix well. Pop the lid on and put it into the fridge. The oats will be ready to eat the next morning, or the morning after that. You will have breakfast ready as soon as you wake up. I like to eat mine with an extra drizzle of honey to make them a little bit sweeter.

This is one of those spur-of-the-moment breakfasts, for when you are unprepared and there's not much in the freezer or fridge—though once you are done with these recipes, you will always have food in the freezer! But for those very occasional days, this is easy, delicious, and pretty quick. It's a really good way of jazzing up the humble baked bean. I'm using naan as my base, but you can use what you like, or simply whatever you have at home.

HARISSA BEAN PIZZA

2 large naan breads
  (or pitas, or leftover bread)

2 x 15-oz/400g cans of
  baked beans

4 teaspoons rose harissa

a handful of baby spinach/
  2 cubes frozen spinach

4 eggs

4 greens onions

Preheat the broiler to medium-high and have a baking sheet at the ready. Place the naan breads on the sheet. Open the cans of beans and get rid of any excess sauce off the top, then pour into a saucepan with the harissa and baby spinach, mix well, and heat gently over medium heat.

Spoon the beans over the surface of each naan, and use the back of your spoon to create 2 little dips for the eggs in each one. Don't be tempted to add too many beans. If you have any left over, just transfer them to a Tupperware container and store them in the fridge, ready to microwave for another meal.

Crack 2 eggs into each naan, then chop the green onions and sprinkle all over the beans and eggs. Don't worry if the egg runs a little.

Cook under the broiler for 5 minutes—this will just set the whites and leave the yolk runny, which is the way I like it. My husband cannot bear to eat runny eggs, so I would broil his for an additional 3 minutes or until the yolk is no longer runny.

Serve and devour straight away.

We love American pancakes but sometimes feel limited as to how often we can have them. Pouring and flipping can take time, so I have taken everything we love about American flavors and Elvis and made this recipe for peanut butter and jelly pancakes, baked all in one and then cut into squares. You can serve them with an extra dollop of jam, some Greek yogurt, and fresh raspberries on the side, if you like.

PEANUT BUTTER AND JELLY SHEETPAN PANCAKE

3 heaped tablespoons jam of your choice (I like a berry jam, because of the deep color and tang, or I just use whatever I happen to have knocking about the house)

3 tablespoons crunchy or smooth peanut butter (or make your own, see p. 246)

cooking oil spray

2 cups/250g all-purpose flour

1 teaspoon baking powder

½ teaspoon salt

3 tablespoons granulated sugar

¾ cup/170ml whole milk

2 large eggs

2 tablespoons vegetable oil

confectioners' sugar, for dusting (if you can be bothered, always looks lovely, takes so little time too)

Start by putting the jam into a microwave-safe bowl and heating it in 10-second bursts, stirring each time until the mixture is simply liquid enough to swirl around—we're not trying to warm it up. Repeat this process with the peanut butter (make sure to avoid putting in too much oil from the jar as this will just make the pancakes greasy). Set both aside.

Preheat the oven to 350°F/180°C. Spray an 8-inch/20cm square baking pan with cooking oil.

Put the flour, baking powder, salt, and sugar into a bowl and whisk together. Make a well in the center and add the milk, along with the eggs and oil. Whisk together until you have a thick batter. If time is even shorter you can make the batter in advance and store it in the fridge overnight.

Pour the batter into the prepared brownie pan and spread out evenly. Take dollops of the jam and spoon them in sporadically, then do the same for the peanut butter. With the end of a spoon, swirl the dollops together slightly to create a marbled effect.

Bake in the oven for about 25 minutes. As soon as the surface of the pancake looks matte and is not wobbly anymore, it is ready. Remove from the oven and cut into squares. Dust with confectioners' sugar, if desired, and serve.

These are great on the go, but you can also freeze any leftover squares in plastic wrap.

MAKES: 20 SQUARES   ACTIVE TIME: 10 MINUTES   TOTAL TIME: 25 MINUTES

I have come to quite like the green stuff. But as a child, very occasionally, I'd remove the pit and fill the avocado with sugar—but the texture wasn't palatable, no matter how much sugar I covered it in. But my goodness, mixed with all sorts of other things, avocado can be transformed, so much so that even my children quite like it. Versatile enough for toast, a dip to go with nachos, or tossed with hot cooked pasta. Just not with sugar!

AVOCADO PESTO

1 small handful of frozen spinach (2½ oz if you want to be precise)

2 small ripe avocados

juice and zest of ½ a lemon

7 tablespoons olive oil

3 cloves of garlic

½ cup walnuts, roughly chopped

1 teaspoon salt

1 teaspoon chile flakes

Put the frozen spinach into the microwave for 1 minute, until it has defrosted. By hand, squeeze out any excess water, then drop the spinach into a blender. Add the avocado flesh, then straight away add the lemon juice and zest to keep any of the beautiful green avocado from going brown.

Add the oil, garlic, walnuts, salt, and chile flakes and blitz until you have a smooth paste. You might need to add 1 or 2 tablespoons of water to help it blend.

You can store the pesto in a jar for 1 week in the fridge. The recipe makes enough for a few meals, so you're already ahead. Freeze in a labeled ziplock bag for up to 3 months.

Turn the page for my favorite ways to serve it.

continued on the next page ➠

MAKES: 1 JAR   TOTAL TIME: 15 MINUTES

AVOCADO PESTO THREE WAYS

WITH CHEESE ON TOAST

Lightly toast 4 slices of bread. Spread 1 tablespoon or so of the avocado pesto on each slice—be as generous or sparing as you like, depending on how much you like the green stuff. Sprinkle with 1 cup of grated cheese and dab with Tabasco. Place under the broiler for 5 minutes, until the cheese is bubbly and melted.

You could have this with a fried egg on the side or just eat it as it is (I quite like it exactly as it is).

WITH NACHOS

2 x 6-oz bags of salted tortilla chips + 1 x 10½-oz jar of hot salsa + 1½ cups grated Cheddar cheese + 1 x 7½-oz jar of jalapeño chiles + ⅔ cup sour cream + fresh cilantro

Preheat the oven to 425°F/220°C.

Spread the tortilla chips across a large baking sheet. Dollop with the hot salsa straight from the jar, then with all of the avocado pesto. Sprinkle with the grated Cheddar on top and bake in the oven for 10 minutes, until the cheese is really melted and crisp.

Remove from the oven and dot with the drained jalapeños. Spoon on the sour cream and finish with a generous sprinkling of chopped cilantro.

WITH PASTA

Cook 9 oz of pasta of your choice (penne, fusilli, etc.) according to the package instructions. Drain, then stir in some of the avocado pesto.

I used to hate sticky rice as a kid, everything from the texture to the taste! But I grew up, revisited it, and never looked back. (Bitter melon I will never revisit and will always hate.) Sticky rice can be so versatile. Cooked with coconut milk, it's rich and creamy, and topped with tempered pineapple, it's even better. If you don't want a second batch in the freezer, simply halve the ingredients.

STICKY COCONUT RICE WITH TEMPERED PINEAPPLE

FOR THE RICE

3¼ cups Thai sticky rice

2 cups cold water

2 x 13.5-oz cans of coconut milk

1 teaspoon salt

FOR THE PINEAPPLE

1 whole pineapple, chopped into chunks, or 2 x 15-oz cans of pineapple chunks, drained (about 1 lb 2 oz drained weight)

2 tablespoons sugar

½ cup plus 2 tablespoons unsalted butter

1 teaspoon crushed caraway seeds

¼ cup unsweetened coconut flakes

TO SERVE

heavy cream

Put the rice into a medium-size (preferably nonstick) pot. Add the water, coconut milk, and salt, and stir.

Place the pot over high heat, and be sure to keep stirring, otherwise the rice will settle on the base and will make that bottom layer stick. Keep moving the rice around. It will start bubbling and spitting furiously. Turn the heat down enough so you are not getting spat at. After about 6 minutes, it should resemble rice pudding—thick, with the grains clearly visible and very milky. Give it one last stir, then remove from the heat. Pop the lid on and let steam for 10 minutes.

Put the pineapple into a heatproof bowl—if you are using canned, be sure to drain off any excess liquid. Add the sugar and mix well.

Place a nonstick frying pan on the stovetop over medium heat and add the butter. As soon as it is melted but not foaming, add the caraway seeds—they will sizzle. Add the coconut flakes and stir until they are golden. Keep stirring gently, watching it carefully.

Now pour the contents of the pan over the pineapple and stir well.

Time to serve. We have made a double helping of the rice, so you don't have to cook it again, just reheat it. Let cool for another time.

To eat now, put some rice into a bowl and top with the pineapple. Apart from tasting delicious, it will make your kitchen smell amazing! Serve with some cream for pouring over the top.

The rice and the pineapple (if you have any left over) can be frozen in separate tubs. Or transform any leftover rice into a dessert (see Burnt Butterscotch Bananas on p. 223).

If I can cook and eat rice for breakfast, that in itself is a luxury for me. It means I have time for at least attempting to slow down. This is a mixture of black and white rice, and so it has a gorgeous color, topped with clotted cream and almond praline.

SLOW COOKER RICE

FOR THE RICE

cooking oil spray

½ cup basmati rice

½ cup black rice

¼ cup butter

¼ cup sugar

2½ cups heavy cream

2½ cups whole milk

1 teaspoon ground nutmeg

FOR THE ALMOND BRITTLE

2 cups sliced almonds

7 tablespoons unsalted
  butter

1 cup sugar

TO SERVE

clotted cream or
  crème fraîche

Spray the slow cooker dish with oil. Put in the two types of rice, the butter, sugar, cream, milk, and nutmeg, then give it a good stir. If you want to cook it faster you can do it for 4 hours on high; if you want it slower you can cook it for 8 hours on low. I do this just before I go to bed so it's ready for when my kids wake at 5 a.m. on a Saturday!

Within the first half hour of cooking be sure to give it a stir, to remove any settled grains of rice.

To make the brittle, have a baking sheet lined with parchment paper ready. Put the almonds into a nonstick pan and toast them over medium heat for about 5 minutes, until they are deep golden. Transfer them to a bowl. Wipe the inside of the pan and pop it back on the heat. Add the butter and sugar and cook, stirring, until the sugar has dissolved. Once it has, increase the heat and continue to boil for 5 minutes, until the caramel is golden. Stir occasionally if there are dark spots.

Add the toasted almonds to the caramel and stir well, then pour the mixture onto the prepared sheet, level it out, and leave to set and harden. When it has set, break off bits of it and crush in a mortar and pestle so that you have uneven chunks and sugary dust and all sorts. Pop into a jar ready for the morning and for plenty of mornings to come.

When the rice is ready, serve with a dollop of chilled clotted cream and the brittle on top. This freezes really well in individual containers, making it perfect for an on-the-go breakfast that can be microwaved. You can also transform any leftovers into a dessert (see Burnt Butterscotch Bananas on p. 223).

SERVES: 12   ACTIVE TIME: 20 MINUTES   TOTAL TIME: 4–8 HOURS

We always knew when my mum was cooking cauliflower curry because that was the only way she cooked cauliflower. The gassy smell would hit us as we came through the door. Never enough to put me off the flowery goodness, though. Everything curried is delicious. But cauliflower doesn't have to be curried or permeate the air with its aroma—this is one of my fave ways to eat it. Hashed, with eggs.

CAULIFLOWER HASH AND EGGS

1 large cauliflower

1 large bunch of fresh chives

1 teaspoon granulated garlic

1 teaspoon salt

½ teaspoon paprika

1 teaspoon cumin seeds

5 tablespoons chickpea flour

vegetable oil, for frying

4 eggs

chile flakes, for sprinkling

Remove the outer leaves from the cauliflower and cut off the stem. Gently pull away as many florets as you can and, if you need to, deploy a knife to cut them away. You'll be left with the leaves and inner core stem. Set these aside—you can prep them for the freezer later.

Grate each floret into a bowl until you have done every single one. For ease you can use a food processor fitted with the coarse grating disk, but if you don't have one, the coarse side of a box grater is ideal.

Finely chop half the chives and add them to the bowl, keeping the other half for drying. Add the garlic granules, salt, paprika, and cumin seeds and mix.

Now add the chickpea flour and stir around to make sure everything is evenly covered. Because each cauliflower differs in size and moisture, you may find that 5 tablespoons of chickpea flour isn't enough. Add 1 tablespoon more flour at a time until the cauliflower looks evenly coated.

Now add water gently in drizzles and mix after each addition. No exact measurement, but you probably need about a cupful. What you are looking for is a mixture that clumps together with no floury bits visible. When the mixture holds together and is not runny, it is perfect.

SERVES: 4   ACTIVE TIME: 30 MINUTES   TOTAL TIME: 50 MINUTES

Drizzle a medium nonstick frying pan with oil so you have a thin, even coating on the base. Place over medium heat, and as soon as the oil is hot add all the cauliflower mixture and flatten it over the base, working it up toward the sides a little too. Let cook for at least 6 to 8 minutes, or until you can see the edges becoming golden.

Use the back of a spoon to create 4 dips in the cauliflower hash. Now, one by one, crack the eggs into the dips, working your way around. I like to avoid the middle, as I serve the hash cut into triangles.

Pop the lid on and cook over low heat for about 10 minutes—this should give you a perfect runny egg, but if you like a firm yolk, leave it on the heat until it is the right runniness or non-runniness for you.

While that is happening, chop the cauliflower leaves and core stem finely, or pulse in a food processor, and put them into a freezer bag. I like to use these for making another hash in the exact same way as above, but using the bits that would otherwise go straight into the compost. They're also good for Spicy Scrap Soup (see p. 77).

Pop the leftover chives into the microwave and give them 10-second bursts until they are totally crisp, then crush them in the palms of your hands.

Serve the hash with a sprinkling of chile flakes and the dried chives you just made. If you've made more than you need, you can put them into a Tupperware container and keep them for another occasion.

Yes, it's spicy food in the morning, but don't be alarmed! Eating spices in the morning was entirely normal growing up. So when I learned from friends that it wasn't normal in every single home in the UK, I don't know who was more horrified—if you like spicy food, you shouldn't be restricted to mealtimes or rules. Give this a go—a little goes a long way, and it's wholesome and delicious and frankly a lot of fun. If you really want to balance things, you could just have toast and marmalade for dinner!

MASALA PORRIDGE

FOR THE PORRIDGE

1⅔ cups rolled oats

1 carrot, grated

1 quart water

1 tablespoon ginger paste

½ teaspoon ground turmeric

1 teaspoon salt

FOR THE TEMPERING

7 tablespoons unsalted butter

1 tablespoon garlic paste

1 teaspoon mustard seeds

TO SERVE

Greek yogurt

chopped fresh cilantro

sunflower seeds

chopped red chiles

Put the oats and grated carrot into a pan, then add the water and stir. Add the ginger paste, turmeric, and salt and stir again. Cook on medium heat for about 15 minutes, until the mixture is thick and bubbling away—if it starts to spit, lower the temperature and be sure to stir occasionally to keep it from sticking.

A few minutes before the end of the porridge cooking time, put the butter into a small frying pan over low heat, and allow to melt. Add the garlic paste, and when it is light brown, add the mustard seeds. As soon as the seeds begin to pop, pour the whole lot straight into the porridge and stir well.

To serve, put a small ladleful into a bowl and add a dollop of yogurt, some cilantro, sunflower seeds, and chopped fresh chile (or dried chile or a grating of frozen chile). If you happen to have any spicy seeds left over from the Thai Red Pepper Soup (see p. 130), you could pop these on top for some extra crunch.

There is enough here to make several single servings that can be microwaved, and this is a great dish to take to work with you, to eat at any time of the day. Store in individual freezer-safe Tupperware containers. Defrost in the fridge, and microwave until piping hot.

SERVES: 6   ACTIVE TIME: 5 MINUTES   TOTAL TIME: 20 MINUTES

Every time I have moved to a new house, or had a baby, or needed to eat fast before an exam, microwave porridge has been my savior, curbing hunger, satisfying, and just getting the job done. But getting the job done can be delicious too. These are my recipes for microwave porridge in four of my favorite flavors. All you need are rolled oats and a food processor. You can make all the flavors here, or simply make the one you want to and work your way through the rest, or better still, come up with your own.

READY BREAKFAST FLAVORED PORRIDGE

11 cups rolled oats, put through the processor enough to break down the oats but not to a fine powder

APPLE AND CINNAMON

6⅓ oz dried apples, cut with scissors into small pieces

2 teaspoons ground cinnamon

BAKEWELL

1 cup mixed dried berries and cherries

4 teaspoons almond extract

1 cup sliced almonds

MANGO AND COCONUT

3½ oz dried mango, chopped

¾ cup dried shredded coconut

1 heaped teaspoon fennel seeds, crushed

CHOCOLATE AND HAZELNUT

⅔ cup unsweetened cocoa powder

⅔ cup chopped roasted hazelnuts

Distribute the oats among four 1-quart airtight jars, 2¾ cups in each.

To make the individual flavors, add the ingredients of your chosen variety to one of your jars of oats and shake around until evenly combined. Or mix in a bowl and then add to the jar.

To make the porridge, the method is the same for all the flavors. Put 6 tablespoons of the flavored oats into a large breakfast bowl and add ¾ cup plus 2 tablespoons of milk of your choice. Be sure to give it a good stir, then pop it into the microwave for 3 minutes.

Let the porridge stand for at least another 3 minutes before you eat it. You can sweeten it however you like—I like to add agave—or you can leave it as it is.

SERVES: 8

ACTIVE TIME: 20 MINUTES PREPPING OATS IN ADVANCE; 5 MINUTES COOKING

Apple and cinnamon   Bakewell

Mango and coconut   Chocolate and hazelnut

As my husband always says, there is nothing wrong with cake for breakfast, and I could not agree more. This has fruit, in the form of prunes, and granola, with a cake in between. All it needs is a good cup of coffee, or strong tea in my case, and that's not a bad way to start the day. Any leftover portions can be frozen.

PRUNEY GRANOLA BAKE

7 tablespoons/100ml buttermilk (but if you don't have buttermilk, which I don't most of the time, you can make your own by adding 1 teaspoon of lemon juice to 7 tablespoons/100ml of whole milk)

3¼ cups/410g dried prunes

½ cup plus 1 tablespoon/ 125g unsalted butter, softened

1 cup/200g sugar

1⅔ cups/200g all-purpose flour

½ teaspoon baking powder

2 large eggs

1 teaspoon vanilla extract

1⅔ cups/200g of your favorite granola (or make your own if you like— see p. 247)

If you are making your own buttermilk, do that now, to allow it time to thicken and do the science bit. Also soak the prunes in 1¼ cups/300ml warm water for about 5 minutes.

Preheat the oven to 350°F/180°C. Grease and line the base of a 9-inch/ 23cm square baking pan and be sure to grease the sides well too.

Drain and roughly chop the prunes, then put them into the pan and spread them out evenly.

Put the butter, sugar, flour, baking powder, eggs, buttermilk, and vanilla into a bowl and give everything a good whisk, using a handheld mixer, until the mixture is super-smooth and shiny—this should only take about 2 minutes. Pour the mixture over the prunes and spread out evenly.

Top with your granola, pressing it gently down onto the batter so it sticks, and bake for 40 to 45 minutes. In the meantime you can get into your first caffeinated beverage.

When the cake is ready, a skewer inserted should come out clean. Let cool in the pan for 5 minutes, then either turn it out or cut it into squares in the pan and scoop it out.

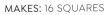

MAKES: 16 SQUARES   ACTIVE TIME: 15 MINUTES   TOTAL TIME: 1 HOUR

My homemade Granola (see p. 247) is fantastic served with ice-cold milk or yogurt, but is also a delicious topping for the Pruney Granola Bake (see p. 43) or used as a layer in my Breakfast Trifle (see p. 47).

Trifle is not just a dessert—it can be eaten for breakfast too. This has as many layers, and is as pleasing to the eye, as a traditional trifle. I have increased the yogurt layer here so that you can make some ice pops or other frozen treats. If you prefer to just make the trifle today, simply halve the quantities in **bold**.

BREAKFAST TRIFLE

FOR THE YOGURT LAYER

3½ cups Greek yogurt

1¼ cups chia seeds

½ cup plus 2 tablespoons honey

2 teaspoons ground cinnamon

FOR THE FRUIT LAYER

3½ cups frozen summer fruits

3 tablespoons confectioners' sugar

1 orange, finely grated zest only (the rest of the orange can be sliced and frozen to use in hot and cold drinks)

FOR THE BREAD/CAKE LAYER

6 oz brioche slices

1½ cups of your favorite granola (or make your own if you like—see p. 247)

FOR THE TOP

whipped cream, from a can

Start by making the chia seed yogurt, so that it can begin to thicken. Put the yogurt into a bowl and stir in the chia seeds, honey, and cinnamon. If you have made the full quantity, place half in one bowl and half in another bowl. Set aside.

Place the frozen fruit in a bowl. Add the confectioners' sugar and orange zest and let the fruit defrost. Drain off the excess juice into a bowl for later. Place the defrosted fruit in the base of your trifle dish.

Rip the brioche into pieces and mix with the granola. Spread in a layer on top of the fruit and drizzle some of the reserved fruit juice over this layer.

Now spoon on the chia yogurt (half, if you have made the full quantity) and allow the trifle to chill in the fridge for 30 minutes. Before serving, squirt on some whipped cream straight from the can.

CHIA AND YOGURT ICE POPS

You can either transfer the remaining chia yogurt into ice pop molds and put into the freezer to set, or add the remaining juice from the defrosted fruit, if you have any left over, and some sliced strawberries and stir well.

Alternatively, you could pop this yogurt into ice cube trays and freeze. Once frozen, transfer to a freezer bag. You now have a base for breakfast smoothies whenever you need them—pop a few cubes into a blender with some kale and pineapple juice, or a banana and berries.

SERVES: 6   ACTIVE TIME: 30 MINUTES   TOTAL TIME: 1 HOUR

I only started to make these after eating store-bought ones out of a package. While those are totally fine, this recipe is a really good way to use up leftover mashed potatoes, but also delicious just to make when you have the time. Any leftovers will freeze well and can be toasted from frozen. I make them with turkey bacon and onions, though pork bacon or vegetarian bacon is just as good, and we like to eat them with pan-roasted tomatoes and scrambled eggs.

TATTY CAKES

FOR THE TATTIES

1 lb 5 oz russet potatoes, peeled, boiled, mashed, and cooled

2 tablespoons vegetable oil

6 pork/turkey/vegetarian bacon slices, cut into strips, optional

1 clove of garlic, crushed

1 small onion, finely chopped

2 teaspoons salt

1 teaspoon black pepper

1 cup all-purpose flour, plus extra for dusting

cooking oil spray

FOR THE ROASTED TOMATO EGGS

6 tablespoons oil

4½ oz cherry tomatoes, halved

½ teaspoon salt

1 teaspoon sugar

1 tablespoon balsamic vinegar

6 eggs, beaten

a handful of fresh parsley/ chives, finely chopped

First make the tatties. Put the cooled mashed potatoes into a bowl and set aside. Heat the oil in a small frying pan. Add the bacon, if using, and cook until golden.

Add the garlic, onion, salt, and pepper and cook for a few minutes, until the onion is soft. Add the mixture to the potatoes and mix well. Now add the flour and mix until you have a stiff dough. Divide into 4 mounds.

Spray a good-sized nonstick frying pan generously with oil and place on medium heat. Flour your work surface, then pat each mound of mixture lightly with the palm of your hand to form a rough circle about ½ inch thick. Cut each circle into 4 triangles.

Cook each triangle for about 4 minutes on each side on low to medium heat. When they are all done, wipe the pan out to make the tomato eggs.

Add the oil to the pan and place on high heat. Add the tomatoes (carefully, as they will splatter). Cook for a couple of minutes, then lower the heat and add the salt, sugar, and balsamic. Cook the tomatoes until they start to soften.

Throw in the eggs and toss them about until they are cooked to your liking. Just before serving with the hot buttered tatties, stir in the parsley/ chives.

SERVES: 4 (WITH SOME EXTRA TATTY CAKES FOR THE FREEZER)   TOTAL TIME: 30 MINUTES

Toad-in-the-hole is not just for dinner; it can be for breakfast too. This is simple and delicious. Sausages, mushrooms, and batter . . . you can't go wrong. I've added some spices to this batter to give an extra punch—and the turmeric gives a lovely vibrancy to the dish.

SAUSAGE AND MUSHROOM TOAD-IN-THE-HOLE

¼ cup/60ml vegetable oil

12 standard-size breakfast sausages of your choice, pierced with a fork

14 oz/400g mushrooms, halved or quartered if large

1 tablespoon coriander seeds, crushed lightly

FOR THE BATTER

1¾ cups/225g all-purpose flour

½ to 1 teaspoon chipotle chile powder

1 tablespoon ground coriander seeds

1 teaspoon ground turmeric

1 teaspoon salt

3 large eggs

1 cup plus 2 tablespoons/ 275ml whole milk

¼ cup/20g crispy fried onions

Preheat the oven to 450°F/240°C.

Put the oil into a 12-inch/30cm round or equivalent size roasting dish. Add the pierced sausages along with the mushrooms, give the dish a jiggle to coat everything with oil, then cook in the oven for about 15 minutes.

To make the batter, put the flour, chipotle chile powder, ground coriander, turmeric, and salt into a bowl and whisk to combine. Make a well in the center and add the eggs and milk, whisking thoroughly to avoid lumps, then stir in the crispy fried onions. If you like, you can make the batter beforehand to save time. You can even make it the day before, but it will thicken overnight, so add a couple of tablespoons of milk and whisk up again if necessary before baking.

Take the dish out of the oven and throw in the crushed coriander seeds—you should hear them sizzle and pop, as the oil will be very hot. Pour the batter around the sausages and put the dish back into the oven to cook for 25 to 30 minutes.

Eat the toad hot, with steak sauce or ketchup. Add a fried egg if you like.

Any leftovers can be frozen, wrapped in parchment paper and foil, and reheated from frozen on a baking sheet lined with foil.

Frying has never scared me—it makes food taste delicious and creates an incredible texture that you can't achieve any other way. As if I didn't like bread enough, fry it and the love just strengthens. Dipping it into the sweet, fruity honey makes this one of my favorite breakfasts.

FRIED BREAD WITH RASPBERRY HONEY

FOR THE BREAD

4 cups/500g bread flour, plus extra for dusting

2 teaspoons salt

1 package (2¼ teaspoons/7g) fast-acting instant yeast

3 tablespoons vegetable oil

1¼ cups/300ml water

vegetable oil, for frying

sea salt flakes, for sprinkling

FOR THE RASPBERRY HONEY

1 cup/350g mild honey

1¼ cups/150g fresh raspberries

TO SERVE

a handful of crushed pistachios (optional)

Put the flour and salt into a mixing bowl. On the other side of the bowl add the yeast and oil, then give it a mix and create a well in the center. Pour the water into the well and gently bring all the ingredients together to form a dough.

Now knead the dough: If you are using a mixer with a dough hook, knead on high speed for 5 minutes. If you are doing it by hand, knead on a lightly floured work surface for 10 minutes. The dough should be stretchy and really shiny. Pop it back into the bowl, cover, and let rise in a warm place for 1 hour, or until the dough has doubled in size.

While the dough is rising, make the raspberry honey. Put the honey into a large bowl. Blitz the raspberries in a blender and then pass them through a fine-mesh sieve to remove the seeds. Pour the raspberry liquid into the honey and mix. Set aside half the raspberry honey to use straight away and put the other half into a jar in the fridge, where it will keep for up to 1 week. Perfect on toast or drizzled over pancakes or just on yogurt.

When the dough has doubled in size, take it out of the bowl and knock it back by giving it a little punch, then divide it into 16 equal balls. Have a baking sheet at the ready, lined with paper towels, and roll out each piece of dough into a circle about ½ inch/1cm thick.

Pop a large frying pan on the stovetop and add oil to reach about ½ inch/1cm up the side. We are shallow-frying, so as the oil depletes, just top it off. Heat the oil on medium for 5 minutes, then slide the first pieces of dough in—they should not touch, so fry two or three at a time, depending on the size of your pan. Fry for 2 minutes on each side.

When the bread is ready, take it out and sprinkle half with sea salt flakes while still hot. This half is for eating now—let the other half cool and freeze for another day.

To make this dish come to life, drizzle some of the raspberry honey over the bread and sprinkle with pistachios. Or eat it the way I do, which is to tear off bits of the bread and dip it into the raspberry honey.

When breakfast is presented as a crown, you feel like you are living your best life. I love placing something right in the center of the table before it is demolished—that brief moment of gasps gives me great pleasure. This looks great, and tastes delicious with the salty tapenade, strong blue cheese, and a hint of rosemary. Not to mention the apricot glaze for sweetness. Any leftovers make a great snack throughout the day, or you can freeze them in slices for another time.

OLIVE AND ROSEMARY CROWN

FOR THE BREAD

2 cups/250g bread flour, plus extra for dusting

1 teaspoon salt

1 package (2¼ teaspoons/7g) fast-acting instant yeast

2 tablespoons dried rosemary

4 tablespoons/50g unsalted butter

½ cup plus 1 tablespoon/ 135ml warm milk

1 large egg, beaten

FOR THE FILLING

½ cup/120g black olive tapenade

5¼ oz/150g blue cheese, crumbled

TO SERVE

3 tablespoons apricot jam, warmed

fresh rosemary leaves, thinly sliced

Put the flour, salt, yeast, dried rosemary, and butter into a bowl, then rub the butter into the flour until it is like breadcrumbs.

Make a well in the center. Add the milk and egg and use your hands to bring the dough together. Knead on a floured surface for 10 minutes, until stretchy and smooth, or if you are using a mixer, knead with a dough hook attached for 5 minutes. Put back into the bowl, cover with plastic wrap, and let rise until it has doubled in size (approx. 1½ hours).

Line a baking sheet with parchment paper. Flour your work surface and tip the dough out. Knock all the air out, then roll the dough into a rectangle about 13 x 10 inches/33 x 25cm. With the long edge facing you, spread the tapenade all over the dough and crumble the blue cheese on top.

Roll the dough up like a jelly roll, as tightly as you can, with the seam at the bottom. Take a knife and cut lengthwise all the way across the center, exposing the swirls and making sure you leave about 1 inch/2.5cm uncut to keep it attached at the very top. You should have what looks like an A that has not been crossed. Turn the cut side out so the layers are visible and simply twist the two pieces, one over the other. Pinch the end and then join the two ends to make a circle. Carefully place on the prepared baking sheet—if you lose the circle shape, now is the time to fix it—then cover with greased plastic wrap and let rise for 30 minutes.

Preheat the oven to 425°F/220°C. When the crown has doubled in size, uncover and bake for 25 minutes. When it is ready, place on a rack to cool.

Warm the jam in the microwave, just enough to loosen it, and brush all over the crown for a beautiful sweet sheen. Sprinkle with fresh rosemary.

You can freeze this loaf, or the leftovers. Cut into slices and pop into a freezer bag.

SERVES: 10

ACTIVE TIME: 30 MINUTES
TOTAL TIME: 3 TO 4 HOURS DEPENDING ON RISING TIME

This uses a simple brioche recipe, but it's stuffed with a banana and chocolate mixture and toasted in a waffle maker. What is great about these waffles is that you can freeze them when they are cool, without the toppings, and simply toast them from frozen. Try different fillings if you like, too—frozen berries, jam, chocolate hazelnut spread …

BANOFFEE WAFFLES

FOR THE WAFFLES

1 cup/240ml warm water

2 teaspoons/6g fast-acting instant yeast

3 tablespoons warm milk

2 tablespoons granulated sugar

3½ cups/450g bread flour, plus extra for dusting

1 teaspoon salt

¼ cup/50g unsalted butter

2 large eggs, beaten

cooking oil spray

FOR THE FILLING

2 ripe bananas, mashed (peeled weight 7 oz/200g)

3½ oz/100g dark chocolate, chips or finely chopped (about ⅔ cup)

1 teaspoon vanilla bean paste

1 tablespoon granulated sugar

TO SERVE

confectioners' sugar, to dust

frozen yogurt or ice cream

crumbled oat cookies

toffee sauce, straight from the bottle

Put the water, yeast, milk, and sugar into a bowl. It should start to froth, which means it's working. Set aside for about 5 minutes.

Put the flour and salt into a second bowl and mix together. Add the butter and rub it in until it is like breadcrumbs. Make a well in the center.

Add the beaten eggs to the yeast mixture, then pour into the center of the dough. Using your hands, get in there and bring the dough together.

Lightly flour a work surface and knead the dough for about 10 minutes. It will be wet, and you may find you need some extra flour to bring it together. You may find it easier to do this using a stand mixer with a dough hook for 10 minutes on medium speed. Pop the dough back into the bowl, cover with a tea towel or plastic wrap, and let rise for 1 hour or until the dough has doubled in size—this will depend on the warmth of your room.

Mix together the mashed banana, chocolate, vanilla, and sugar to make the filling, then cover and place in the fridge.

Have a floured baking sheet at the ready. When the dough has doubled in size, take it out of the bowl and knock it back on a floured surface. By which I mean get your fingers and knuckles in and squash it back down. Divide it into 12 balls. Take the filling out of the fridge. Flatten each bit of dough and lay them out on the surface.

Divide the filling between the 12 bits of dough, then take each one and pinch the dough into the center to encase the filling. Pinch the edges hard to seal, then pop them onto the prepared baking sheet seam-side down. Cover and let rest as you prepare your toppings.

Turn the waffle maker on and spray generously with oil. Pop a dough ball into the center and push the iron down. Cook for 3 to 5 minutes, or until the waffle has a crisp, golden exterior.

If eating straight away, dust with confectioner's sugar and add your toppings. Be generous, be frivolous, and go high!

This bread is so easy to make and has all the delicious flavors of a spotted dick, the traditional British pudding. Bread making can be fun and does not have to be laborious. Spotted dick can take a long time to make what with the steaming, but this way you can have those delicious flavors without spending all your time in the kitchen. This is a great time to make your own butter too, seeing as you will have all that spare time.

SPOTTED DICK BREAD WITH HOMEMADE BUTTER

FOR THE BREAD

1⅔ cups/400ml buttermilk (if you have no buttermilk, you can make your own by adding 2 tablespoons of lemon juice to 1⅔ cups/ 400ml of whole milk)

4 cups/500g all-purpose flour

1 teaspoon salt

2 tablespoons sugar

1 teaspoon baking soda

¼ cup/50g vegetable shortening

1⅓ cups/100g candied citrus peel

¾ cup/100g currants

1 orange, finely grated zest only (slice the rest and pop it into a freezer bag for extra flavor in cold drinks)

1 lemon, finely grated zest only (slice as above)

FOR THE BUTTER

2½ cups/600ml heavy cream

1 tablespoon sea salt

If you're making your own buttermilk, now is the time to do it, to give it time to thicken and do its sciencey thing!

Preheat the oven to 425°F/220°C and line a baking sheet with parchment paper.

Put the flour, salt, sugar, baking soda, shortening, candied peel, currants, and citrus zest into a bowl and mix really well. Make a little well in the center and pour in your buttermilk, using a spatula to bring the mixture together. Tip it out onto a work surface and gently bring the dough together, without kneading it—you don't want to overwork it. Place it onto the baking sheet and flatten it down, then use a knife to make 4 cuts all the way through, to create 8 triangles. Bake in the oven for 30 minutes.

While it's baking, make the butter. Put the cream into a mixer, or use a handheld mixer, and whisk. It will quickly get to stiff peaks—just keep it going and then it will separate. This is exactly what you want. As soon as it does that it will change fast—you will be able to hear it. There will be a lot of sloshing, where the water separates from the fat. What you should be left with is crumbly-looking butter and liquid in the bottom of the bowl.

Have ready a colander lined with cheesecloth, or a thin piece of cotton. Tip the butter into the colander and place it in the sink for all that excess liquid to drain off. As the dripping slows down, give it a good squeeze to get rid of some more moisture. Add the salt and mix well, then set aside the amount you need for the bread and refrigerate the rest. It will keep in the fridge for 1 month.

When the bread comes out of the oven, let it cool on a rack for 15 minutes, if you can resist the urge not to eat it straight away. Then pull away the triangular wedges of warm bread and spread them with your fresh butter.

If you have any bread left over, slice it and freeze it. You can pop it straight into the toaster from frozen.

SERVES: 8   ACTIVE TIME: 30 MINUTES   TOTAL TIME: 1 HOUR

I think sliders are just burgers really, and as much as I like making them, I never seem to make the same version twice—when I really like one it always tastes different the next time, so I always make these large sliders in twelves. That way we have the same thing each time and it all kind of happens in one pan. We love them for breakfast, but you can add a salad and turn them into lunch, or add fries and make them into dinner.

SAUSAGE AND EGG SLIDERS

vegetable oil, for greasing

12 sausages

2 tablespoons granulated onion

1 teaspoon granulated garlic

12 large eggs

1 tablespoon chipotle chile flakes

salt and pepper

12 regular-sized burger buns, batch baked so they're joined together (or 2 x 6, whatever you can find)

unsalted butter, for spreading

12 slices of cheese (I like the stuff wrapped individually in cellophane)

sauce of your choice (I like steak sauce)

Preheat the oven to 425°F/220°C and make sure you have a roasting dish large enough to fit all 12 buns comfortably or 2 rimmed baking sheets that each fit 6. Grease the inside of the dish really well and line with parchment paper.

Take the sausages out of their skins and place in a large bowl, then mix in the onion and garlic granules. Squash each bit of sausage meat into the roasting dish until you have covered the base, then bake in the oven for 10 minutes.

Meanwhile, whisk the eggs well and season with the chipotle flakes, salt, and pepper. Take the roasting dish out of the oven and transfer the sausage meat to a baking sheet. Grease the roasting dish again, really well. Pour in the eggs, making sure they reach all the corners. Bake for 5 minutes, then take the eggs out and place on top of the sausage meat on the baking sheet.

Slice the buns in a clean sweep horizontally and take off the tops. Spread the bases with butter and pop them into the roasting dish. Lay the sausage meat and eggs on top, cut around each bun, then add the 12 slices of cheese. Squeeze steak sauce or ketchup or both on the cheese. Put the tops back on the buns and put back into the oven for just 5 minutes, to warm the bread and melt the cheese.

Freeze individual sliders in plastic wrap.

Eggs are by far my favorite things to cook and eat. Not simply for their versatility but also for their ability to take on any flavor—we can make omelets with them and bake cakes with them, and you can't get much more flexible than that. These rolls are lovely—the eggs glue themselves to the tortillas, so that they are easy as pie to roll, making them delicious and portable. They freeze really well, too, for a breakfast on the go and a makeshift lunch box cooler all at the same time.

EGG ROLLS

6 large eggs

1 tablespoon dried parsley

1 teaspoon granulated garlic

½ teaspoon salt

½ teaspoon black pepper

vegetable oil, for frying

⅔ cup sliced black olives (drained from a 6½-oz jar)

3½ oz fresh, frozen, or canned button mushrooms, sliced (optional)

6 small flour or corn tortillas

6 teaspoons sun-dried tomato paste

Crack the eggs into a bowl, then add the parsley, garlic granules, salt, and pepper and give everything a good mix.

Put a small nonstick frying pan (8 or 9 inches, to be precise) on the stovetop on medium heat, and drizzle in 2 teaspoons of oil.

Take the time at this stage to peel your tortillas away from each other; otherwise you will be frustrated when you can't get them separated, and frustration leaves you with big holes in your tortillas.

Put the olives into a bowl and the sliced mushrooms, if using, in another bowl, and have them nearby. Pour 3 tablespoons of the egg mixture into the pan—the eggs should sizzle, but if they don't, turn the heat up a little. Scatter a few olive slices and mushrooms over the wet egg mix.

Take a tortilla and spread it with a teaspoon of sun-dried tomato paste. Quickly put the tortilla on top of the egg, paste side down. While the wrap and egg are cooking, get the next tortilla ready, spread with the paste.

Using the back of a slotted spatula, press the top of the tortilla to help distribute the egg under the wrap. Cook for no more than 30 seconds, then, as soon as the egg has glued itself to the tortilla, flip over and cook on the other side just to warm it through for another 30 seconds.

Take the pan off the heat and put the tortilla/egg on a plate. Roll the whole thing when it is cool enough to touch. Do the same with the rest of the wraps until the egg is used up.

Wrap any leftovers in plastic wrap and pop them into the freezer.

When you are ready to eat the leftovers, let thaw in the fridge. Or microwave with plastic wrap still on for 1 minute on high, until hot all the way through. Keep heating in 10 second bursts, if needed.

SERVES: 6   TOTAL TIME: 20 MINUTES

I love making this—the muffins are filled with tangy sun-dried tomato and cheese, covered with a cheesy sauce, and baked. It's warm and wonderful and there is a double helping of sauce to freeze for a macaroni and cheese another time (see Box below, or just halve the **bold** sauce ingredients if you don't want to do this).

ENGLISH MUFFIN BAKE

FOR THE CHEESE SAUCE

¼ cup/60g unsalted butter

½ cup/60g all-purpose flour

5 cups/1.2L whole milk

½ teaspoon salt

1 tablespoon nutritional yeast

3½ oz/100g Cheddar cheese, grated

FOR THE ENGLISH MUFFINS

7 English muffins

½ cup plus 2 tablespoons sun-dried tomato paste

3½ oz/100g Cheddar cheese, grated

Preheat the oven to 425°F/220°C and have a 9 x 5-inch/900g loaf pan at the ready.

Melt the butter in a pan, then add the flour and whisk into a smooth paste. Pour in the milk a little at a time, making sure to keep mixing—the mixture needs to come back to a boil before each milk addition. Cook on low heat for 5 minutes, then take off the heat. Stir in the salt and nutritional yeast, then add the cheese and stir well.

Toast the muffins and slice them in half. Spread both cut sides with the sun-dried tomato paste and sprinkle with a little of the cheese, then sandwich them back together. Spread a little cheese sauce in the bottom of the loaf pan. Line the muffins up next to each other in the pan and pour half of the remaining sauce all over them, making sure you get the sauce into all the gaps. Top with the rest of the cheese and bake for 30 minutes, until the top is really crisp.

MACARONI AND CHEESE

You can freeze the rest of the cheese sauce for another time, or make macaroni and cheese now so that you have a dinner to eat at some point in the next few days. Cook 9 oz/250g of macaroni and drain, then add to the sauce and stir well. Pour into an ovenproof freezer-safe dish, and sprinkle with grated cheese. Let cool, then freeze until needed. To cook, preheat the oven to 400°F/200°C and bake uncovered for 40 minutes.

SERVES: 4–6   ACTIVE TIME: 30 MINUTES   TOTAL TIME: 1 HOUR

These are like crumpets, but thinner and with no need for a special mold to make them. They are satisfying to make as you watch the bubbles come to the surface. These are made with cocoa, so they have a subtle chocolate flavor. Served with whipped butter—yes!

COCOA PIKELETS WITH WHIPPED MAPLE BUTTER

FOR THE PIKELETS

4 cups/500g bread flour

⅔ cup/50g cocoa powder

1 package (2¼ teaspoons/7g) fast-acting instant yeast

2 teaspoons sugar

1½ cups/350ml warm water

1½ cups/350ml whole milk

cooking oil spray

FOR THE WHIPPED MAPLE BUTTER

½ cup plus 2 tablespoons/ 150g butter, softened

8 teaspoons maple syrup

Begin by making the pikelets. Put the flour and cocoa powder into a bowl, then stir in the yeast and sugar. Now add the water and milk, and whisk to bring the whole thing together into a smooth paste. Cover and let rise in a warm place until it has doubled in size and is bubbly.

While that happens, make the whipped butter. Put the butter into a small bowl along with 2 teaspoons of the maple syrup. Whip for 2 minutes on high, then pop into the freezer for 2 minutes.

Now take the butter out, add another 2 teaspoons of maple syrup, and whip for another 2 minutes. Then put back into the freezer for 2 minutes. Take it out again, add 2 more teaspoons of maple syrup and whip for another 2 minutes. Then put back into the freezer, again, for 2 minutes.

Then for the last time, take it out, add the remaining 2 teaspoons of maple syrup, whip, and pop into a serving dish.

Once the dough has doubled in size, spray a nonstick frying pan with oil and place on medium heat. Put 2 tablespoons of the dough mix into the pan to form each pikelet. They shouldn't touch while cooking, so you may have to do this in several batches to avoid crowding the pan. Cook gently for 2 minutes, or until the surface looks dry and matte. Then turn them over and cook for 30 seconds.

The pikelets are best eaten warm with copious amounts of the whipped butter, or cold later. Freeze between layers of parchment paper and pop into a freezer bag.

MAKES: 30   ACTIVE TIME: 30 MINUTES   TOTAL TIME: 1 HOUR 45 MINUTES

Scones are one of the first things most kids learn to bake, especially in high school. So varying them is a load of fun, and to have them for breakfast is even better. These are cheesy and spread with a delicious mustardy paste.

PARMESAN SCONES WITH SALMON PASTE

FOR THE PARMESAN SCONES

4 cups/500g all-purpose flour

½ cup/110g unsalted butter, cubed

2 tablespoons baking powder

½ teaspoon salt

1 teaspoon granulated onion

1 tablespoon dried chives

½ cup/50g grated Parmesan cheese, plus a little extra for sprinkling

1¼ cups/300ml whole milk

1 egg, beaten

FOR THE SALMON PASTE

4½ oz/120g smoked salmon trimmings

1 tablespoon whole-grain mustard

½ teaspoon salt

a sprinkling of ground black pepper

5 tablespoons/75g Greek yogurt or crème fraîche

Preheat the oven to 425°F/220°C. Lightly grease two baking sheets.

Put the flour and butter into a bowl and rub together with your fingertips until it is like breadcrumbs. Add the baking powder, salt, onion granules, chives, and cheese and mix really well. Make a well in the center and pour in all the milk, then bring the dough together into one large mound.

Roll the dough out on a flour-dusted work surface to a thickness of ¾ inch/2cm, making sure to keep it to a rectangular shape. Using a sharp knife, cut it into 18 squares and place them on the baking sheets about 1 inch/2.5cm apart. Brush with egg, sprinkle with Parmesan, and bake till golden on top, 12 to 15 minutes. Switch the position of the sheets halfway through for even baking.

To make the salmon paste, put the salmon, mustard, salt, pepper, and yogurt into a blender and blitz.

When the scones are ready, put them on a rack to cool. Freeze half of them in bags and eat the other half spread with the salmon paste.

This is like meatloaf meets Wellington meets sausage roll. Which can never really be a bad thing. With a line of hard-boiled eggs hidden inside, it's delicious for breakfast but also wonderful, cold sliced, between a soft, floury, heavily buttered bun. Makes a great snack throughout the day—and it's perfect for picnics.

MEATLOAF ROLL

1 lb 2 oz/500g lean ground beef

6 sausages, taken out of their skins

1 teaspoon chile flakes

1 teaspoon salt

2 cloves of garlic, crushed

1 small onion, finely chopped

1 slice of bread, blitzed into breadcrumbs, or 5 tablespoons dried breadcrumbs

a large handful of fresh parsley

5 hard-boiled eggs (boiled for 8 minutes, then plunged into cold water), peeled

1 lb 2 oz/500g defrosted puff pastry

1 tablespoon nutritional yeast, mixed with 1 teaspoon warm water

1 egg, beaten

Preheat the oven to 400°F/200°C.

Put the ground beef, sausage meat, chile flakes, salt, garlic, onion, and breadcrumbs into a bowl and mix together with your hands. Add the parsley and mix until you have flecks of green all through the meat mixture.

Place two long lengths of plastic wrap on your work surface, one overlapping the other. Turn the meat mixture onto it and pat it out with damp hands into a rectangular shape about 12 x 10 inches/30 x 25cm. Line up the hard-boiled eggs in a row down the center of the rectangle, short end to short end. With the aid of the plastic wrap, create a large sausage shape. The eggs should be encased by the meat, rather like a long Scotch egg. Twist the ends of the plastic wrap and put the roll into the fridge.

Meanwhile, roll out the pastry to about 14 x 14 inches/35 x 35cm and ¼-inch/5mm thickness. Brush the surface with the yeast mixture. Remove the meat roll from the plastic wrap and place lengthwise on the rolled-out pastry, just off center. Bring the larger side of the pastry over the meat roll, then pinch the edges together to close. Crimp all the way around.

Brush the pastry with the egg wash and place on a baking sheet. Put it into the preheated oven and bake for about 1 hour, or until the pastry is golden and the roll is cooked through.

TO GET AHEAD

If you want to get ahead, you can prepare all this the night before and bake it in the morning. After brushing the roll with the egg wash, wrap it in plastic and place it in the fridge on its baking sheet overnight. The following morning, preheat the oven to 400°F/200°C, remove the plastic wrap, and cook the roll for 45 minutes. Decrease the oven temperature to 350°F/180°C and bake for 30 minutes more, or until cooked through.

SERVES: 8

ACTIVE TIME: 1 HOUR   TOTAL TIME: 2 HOURS

LUNCH

I love anything where as little cooking as possible is required—not because I don't like cooking, it's just that sometimes I don't want to do it. All you need for this is a blender, smoothie maker, or food processor—whatever you use to make mush will work, and the only cooking is the pasta. This tastes delicious, but my goodness, the color! This recipe will give you two portions of the glorious beet sauce, but if you just want to make a single batch today, halve the ingredients in **bold**.

BLENDER BEETS

1 lb 2 oz pasta

1 lb 5 oz cooked beets, drained

7 tablespoons olive oil, plus extra for serving

1 teaspoon fine salt

4 cloves of garlic

1 large red chile (seeded if you don't want it too spicy)

7 oz feta cheese

1 cup fresh dill, finely chopped

1 tablespoon lemon juice, fresh or out of a bottle

Cook the pasta as per the instructions on the package.

Meanwhile, make the sauce. Put the beets into a blender and add the olive oil, salt, garlic, and chile. Blend to a smooth paste.

Put half the sauce into a small ziplock freezer bag, seal, and freeze. Now you have another batch of the sauce ready for another meal.

Crumble the feta cheese and place in a bowl. Chop the dill and add to the cheese, then drizzle in the lemon juice and mix.

Once the pasta is cooked to your liking (I like it a little bit firm), drain and put back into the pan. Pour in all that beautiful beet sauce and mix well. I can't help but be mesmerized by nature when the color mixes with the pasta, staining it bright pink.

Tip it out onto a serving dish and sprinkle with all the feta and dill mix. Drizzle with a little extra oil for good measure before serving.

The frozen sauce will keep for up to 6 months. Store in a labeled ziplock bag.

SERVES: 5   TOTAL TIME: 10 MINUTES

I never ate these freezer-aisle equivalents until I made a trip to a specialty freezer supermarket. I absolutely loved them! But as with most things, I dissected them and made my own version, with no less than three cheeses and a dip to go with them. We make 8 here, which will either serve 4 very hungry people, or you can pop a few in the freezer to have your own homemade version ready as instantly as the store-bought variety!

THREE CHEESE CRISPY PANCAKES

FOR THE CRISPY PANCAKES

1 cup plus 2 tablespoons/ 250g mascarpone

2 tablespoons whole milk

5¼ oz/150g any hard cheese (I like a combo of red Leicester, sharp Cheddar, and Parmesan)

2 cloves of garlic, crushed

1 medium red onion, chopped

8 store-bought crêpe pancakes

4 large eggs, beaten

2¾ cups/300g seasoned breadcrumbs

cooking oil spray

FOR THE SAUCE

1 x 7½-oz/215g jar of jalapeños, drained

5 tablespoons/75ml olive oil

a pinch of salt

a small handful of fresh mint leaves

Mix the mascarpone with the milk and blend to a smooth paste. Stir in the cheese, garlic, and chopped onion.

Have ready a baking sheet that fits in the freezer. Lay out the pancakes on a work surface and divide the filling mixture among the centers. Brush the edges very lightly with some of the beaten egg, then fold them over and press together to create semicircles, firmly so they stick together. Flatten them a bit with your hand, then place on the sheet and put them straight into the freezer. To save space, you can freeze one layer of pancakes on top of the other, with sheets of parchment paper in between.

Preheat the oven to 400°F/200°C and have two greased baking sheets ready. Have the whisked eggs ready in a shallow dish and the breadcrumbs on another. Take the pancakes out of the freezer, dip them into the egg and then into the breadcrumbs, then pop them onto the baking sheets. Press down and really push the crumbs into the egg so they stick. Spray the pancakes generously with oil and bake for 30 minutes, until crisp and golden.

To make the sauce, put the jalapeños, oil, salt, and mint into a blender and whiz to a smooth sauce. I like to use the sauce as a drizzle over a simple leaf salad or just as a dip.

Once cooked, the pancakes can be frozen.

For a quick meal, quesadillas are my favorite thing to make when I have roast chicken left over from Sunday dinner. But I always have roasted chicken breasts in the freezer—you can buy them by the bagful—something that was my saving grace a few years ago when we were ferrying the kids between one after-school activity and the next. This is what I love to do with leftover or precooked chicken, keeping it fresh with the flavors of tzatziki and adding cheese to melt the quesadillas together—they are firmly up there as a total fave in our house.

TZATZIKI QUESADILLAS

12¼ oz roasted chicken breast, sliced (or scraps off a roasted chicken carcass)

½ cucumber, grated

2 tablespoons Greek yogurt

1 teaspoon dried mint

1 teaspoon granulated garlic

2 teaspoons za'atar (you can find this with the spices in the supermarket aisle)

½ teaspoon salt

4½ oz Cheddar cheese, grated

1 x 7½-oz jar of jalapeños, drained

5 large flour tortillas

cooking oil spray

Put the chicken into a bowl. Squeeze any excess juice out of the grated cucumber and add to the bowl, then stir in the yogurt, mint, garlic granuals, za'atar, salt, and cheese. Chop the jalapeños and stir into the chicken mix.

Spread the filling over one half of each tortilla, making sure to spread it all the way to the edge, then fold over.

Pop a griddle pan on medium heat and spray it with oil. Cook one tortilla at a time, using a slotted spatula to press down so the cheese melts and helps to stick the wrap together. Cook for 3 minutes on each side.

If you are serving these at a get-together, let them cool slightly and cut them into smaller triangles, but otherwise just cut them in half and serve.

Leftovers freeze well, and can be heated from frozen.

The filling can be kept in the fridge for 5 days and is great with a baked potato if you don't fancy quesadillas again.

SERVES: 5   TOTAL TIME: 45 MINUTES

This lentil and orange combo is one of my favorites. Lentils were a staple when I was growing up and they still are. I love them, and so do my children, so I have found loads of ways of cooking them, some traditional and others a bit less traditional. They work brilliantly to thicken up a soup. And once a soup is made, you have one of the quickest lunches all ready to go in your fridge or freezer.

LENTIL AND ORANGE SOUP

1½ cups split red lentils

2 quarts cold water

1 teaspoon baking powder

2 teaspoons ground turmeric

1½–2 teaspoons salt

1–2 teaspoons chile flakes

½ cup plus 2 tablespoons vegetable oil

8 cloves of garlic, crushed

2 teaspoons coriander seeds, crushed

finely grated zest and juice of 2 large oranges

TO SERVE

fresh cilantro

heavy cream, to drizzle

crusty bread

Put the lentils into a large saucepan, then wash and rinse them until the water runs clear. Drain, then put them back into the saucepan and add the cold water.

Add the baking powder—this helps to retain a bold color. Add the turmeric, salt, and chile flakes. Stir them, otherwise they will all just sit on the surface. Pop the pan on to high heat and bring to a boil, stirring all the time. You have to stir to prevent the lentils from sticking in the first place. As soon as it has boiled, keep it on medium heat to simmer away.

After half an hour, put the oil into a small pan over high heat, then add the garlic and cook till golden brown. Add the coriander seeds and as soon as they start to pop, pour the mixture into the lentils and stir well.

To finish, add the orange zest and juice and simmer for another 5 minutes. Take off the heat and serve with chopped cilantro, a drizzle of cream, and some crusty bread.

If you have any soup left over you can let it cool, then put it into individual portions in Tupperware containers and freeze.

I have been saving scraps for as long as I can remember. I started when I began weaning my second little boy. I needed to save money and we had to find ways to waste less, eat comfortably, and not be totally short at the end of the month. It seemed mindless to throw away these beautiful peelings, the most nutritious and delicious part of most root veg, full of flavor and full of fiber, and it helped my conscience as well as my wallet. The scraps developed from baby foods to peelings I would deep-fry to soup. This recipe varies and changes, but each time we end up with a hearty, healthy soup that could have otherwise ended up in the compost.

SPICY SCRAP SOUP

1½ lb frozen scraps (potato peel, parsnip peel, carrot peel, broccoli/cauliflower stalks, you get the idea…)

1 tablespoon chile flakes

3 tablespoons granulated onion

2 tablespoons granulated garlic

2 tablespoons salt

2 lemons, juice and finely grated zest

¼ cup dried cilantro (that's a whole jar)

2 quarts of vegetable stock

1 slice of bread

TO SERVE

Greek yogurt

fresh chives

Tip out the frozen peelings into a large stockpot.

Add the chile flakes, onion and granulated garlic, the salt, lemon zest and juice, and dried cilantro.

Add the stock and rip slices of the bread into the pot. The bread is what gives it a lovely creamy texture.

Pop the pot on high heat and bring everything to a rapid boil. As soon as it has boiled, lower the heat and keep on medium heat. With the lid on, allow it to cook for at least 1½ to 2 hours till everything in the pan is soft and falling apart. By this point it should start to look less like peelings.

Take it off the heat and blitz using an immersion blender till you have a smooth soup. If you're eating this or making it for the family, pat yourself on the back for making soup—hot, delicious, and nutritious—out of peelings, food waste, potential compost. A wholesome meal. If you're serving this to friends, ask them what they think went into it. I reckon they won't be able to guess!

To serve, add a dollop of Greek yogurt and a small sprinkling of freshly scissored chives.

Once cooled, it can be portioned and frozen.

Instant noodles are my favorite thing when I need comfort food—they're easy, simple to make, and so versatile. They can be eaten as they are or jazzed up to be a bit more special, either with extra chile sauce or bulked up with some vegetables. By making my own, I'm never short on noodles when I run out of the foil packet variety. I've given the ingredients for four variations—these are the ones I enjoy the most, using up things I tend to have at home. You'll need a selection of pint jars with lids—each variation makes one jar. And get your measuring cups out, because we're making a big batch of spice paste to last.

INSTANT NOODLES

FOR THE SPICE PASTE

3 medium onions, quartered

2 heads of garlic, peeled

7 tablespoons vegetable oil

½ cup balsamic vinegar

½ cup plus 2 tablespoons fish sauce

½ cup plus 2 tablespoons light soy sauce

½ cup brown sugar

¾ cup plus 1 tablespoon chile paste

FOR THE NOODLES

1½ oz instant noodles (per portion) of your choice

To make the spice paste, blitz the onions and garlic in a food processor until pulsed but not a smooth paste.

Put the oil into a pan on medium heat. When it's hot, add the onions and garlic and cook for 10 to 15 minutes, until the onions are brown. Now add the vinegar, fish sauce, soy sauce, brown sugar, and chile paste, and cook until the mixture is a thick paste with no liquid. This should take about 20 minutes on medium to low heat.

When the spice paste is cooked and cooled, put it into a jar—it should keep in the fridge for 2 months.

Now to make the noodles. Put 1 tablespoon of the spice paste into a pint jar, along with your portion of noodles and all the other bits. Store it in the fridge, and when you are ready to eat, pour 1¼ cups of boiling water into the jar and pop the lid on. I like my noodles brothy, but if you like a drier noodle, just add less water. These are great for home but also perfect for taking to work.

continued on the next page ➥

SERVES: 1 PERSON; PASTE MAKES ENOUGH FOR 4–8   TOTAL TIME: 35 MINUTES

NOODLE VARIATIONS

CHICKEN AND PEA

1 tablespoon spice paste (see p. 78) + 3 tablespoons frozen peas + 3 table-spoons frozen onions + a small handful of cooked chicken + ¼ of a lime, squeezed, then dropped into the jar + 1 teaspoon dried dill

BEEF AND KIMCHI

1 tablespoon spice paste + 1 green onion, sliced + 1 tablespoon kimchi + 2 strips of beef jerky, thinly cut with scissors + ½ teaspoon smoked paprika

SOY MUSHROOM

1 tablespoon spice paste + ½ x 10-oz can of sliced mushrooms, drained + ¼ cup texturized vegetable protein, dried or frozen + 1 cube of frozen spinach + a slice of lemon, squeezed and dropped into the jar

EGG NOODLES

1 tablespoon spice paste + ¼ cup mixed frozen veg + 2 eggs, cracked straight into the jar + 1 tablespoon coriander seeds, crushed + 1 teaspoon dried dill

While the pastry is perhaps my favorite part of a quiche, occasionally, for me, removing one element of a dish makes life just a little bit quicker but still delicious all the same. I love making this because for the most part I have all the ingredients at home. Full of spinach, it fills me with joy—as does anything bright green. It's good eaten straight away, but is even better chilled and eaten later.

CRUSTLESS SPINACH QUICHE

butter, for greasing

3½ oz/100g frozen spinach, defrosted

1 teaspoon ginger paste

1 teaspoon chile flakes

½ teaspoon salt

¼ teaspoon ground turmeric

5¼ oz/150g extra-sharp Cheddar cheese, grated

6 large eggs, beaten

1⅔ cups/400ml whole milk

plain yogurt, to serve

Preheat the oven to 425°F/220°C. Generously grease a 9-inch/23cm pie dish.

Put the spinach into a medium bowl, first squeezing out any excess water by pressing it between two sheets of paper towel. Mix in the ginger paste, chile flakes, salt, and turmeric, then add the cheese, eggs, and milk and mix well, using a fork as this helps separate the spinach.

Pour into the prepared dish and bake in the oven for 30 to 35 minutes. You will know it is cooked when there is no longer a wobble in the center.

Take out of the oven and let cool for at least 15 minutes before cutting—this will give it just enough time to set, making it easier to cut. I like to serve it simply with some yogurt.

SERVES: 4–6   ACTIVE TIME: 20 MINUTES   TOTAL TIME: 1 HOUR

To be totally honest, you can make anything taste good if you add salty cheese or melted sugar, but when you do the two together, it becomes a taste explosion in your mouth. This is bread topped with an easy chile-pecan paste that can be used in so many different ways, but the paste spread on some bread and topped with slices of Brie, sprinkled with sugar, and then broiled, is especially yummy. Make the paste and you can use it on other things, but first try it with some crunchy, sweet broiled Brie.

PECAN BRIE BRÛLÉE

2 cups pecans

5 tablespoons vegetable oil

4 teaspoons chile paste

1 teaspoon granulated garlic

a pinch of salt

4 slices of bread (sourdough
  would be nice)

7 oz Brie cheese

2 tablespoons Demerara sugar

To make the chile-pecan paste, put the pecans into a food processor and blitz until totally ground. Gradually add the oil—the mixture should begin to come together. Now add the chile paste, garlic granules, and salt.

Turn the broiler to high.

Spread half the chile-pecan paste in an even layer over the bread slices and put them on a baking sheet. Cut the Brie into slices and put them on top of the pecan paste. Sprinkle with the sugar and place under the broiler until it has caramelized. This should only take 5 minutes, but it can vary depending on your broiler.

Put the remainder of the chile-pecan paste into a jar. It will keep in the fridge for up to 1 month. You can use it on toast or cookies—I enjoy it spread on salty crackers when I'm peckish in the middle of the night. Or see below for how to use it as a sauce for a delicious chicken dish.

CHILE-PECAN CHICKEN WITH RICE

Mix the leftover paste with 1¼ cups heavy cream, along with the finely grated zest and juice of 2 limes. Cook 2 chicken breasts in a pan with some oil, and as soon as the chicken is browned all over, add the nut-cream mixture and cook with the lid on for 10 minutes on low heat. Perfect with some steamed veg or a package of microwave rice.

SERVES: 4   TOTAL TIME: 20 MINUTES

Eggplants are totally delicious, but I always think they feel like more effort than they are worth when you watch them being salted, left to drain, etc. Mum always just threw them into a curry, but there is a faster way to eat them. The microwave is my friend—you can cook them in the little box of wonder and this is how. The sauce is really versatile, too.

ASIAN EGGPLANT WEDGES

3 tablespoons dark soy sauce

2 tablespoons balsamic vinegar

2 tablespoons vegetable oil

1 teaspoon garlic paste

1 teaspoon ginger paste

1 teaspoon chile paste or gochujang paste

2 tablespoons honey

2 medium eggplants

TO SERVE

a small handful of fresh cilantro, chopped

1 red chile, thinly sliced

1 tablespoon sesame seeds

Start by making the marinade. Put the soy sauce, balsamic, oil, garlic paste, ginger paste, chile paste, and honey into a microwaveable medium bowl.

Remove the stalks from the eggplants, then cut each one into 8 wedges. Throw them all into the bowl of marinade and toss them around. If you can bear it, allow the eggplants to sit and soak up the mixture for at least 5 minutes. You can wait and watch, or make a cup of tea, or chop the cilantro and chile.

Cover the bowl with plastic wrap and cook in the microwave on your highest setting for 13 minutes.

When the bowl comes out it will be hot, so be careful. Carefully remove the plastic and put the eggplants on a plate. Sprinkle with the cilantro, chile, and sesame seeds.

I would normally set aside whatever is left over and use it as part of a salad the next day—you could do that, or you could eat it all now.

STIR-FRIED NOODLES

You can also use this marinade as a stir-fry sauce for noodles or serve it with egg fried rice. Cook 2 nests of noodles following the package instructions. Drain, then return the noodles to the saucepan with the eggplant sauce and cook for 1 to 2 minutes, tossing to coat the noodles.

SERVES: 2–4   ACTIVE TIME: 10 MINUTES   TOTAL TIME: 25 MINUTES

Chicken breast can be dry and it's not always my protein of choice—bit of lamb any day! But enough sauce can really transform it, and packing the marinara with lots of flavor is important. Also, this is my creamy version mixed with hummus, because I always have a stray tub at the end of the week, and it works beautifully in this. We're going to make a double batch here so that you have another meal for 4 in the freezer, but if you prefer to just make enough for today, simply halve all of the ingredients.

CREAMY MARINARA CHICKEN

FOR THE CHICKEN

8 chicken breasts

2 cups/500g uncooked tomato purée

1 tablespoon granulated onion

1 tablespoon dried basil

1 tablespoon dried oregano

1½ teaspoons salt

1 teaspoon ground black pepper

½ x 7-oz/198g jar of capers (about ½ cup/65g capers, drained weight)

3 tablespoons olive oil

2 tablespoons hummus

FOR THE COUSCOUS

1 medium zucchini

2⅓ cups couscous

1 chicken bouillon cube, crushed

1 x 15-oz/400g can of chickpeas, drained

2 tablespoons basil pesto

7 tablespoons/100ml olive oil

Cut a horizontal slit in each chicken breast, then tease open to allow lots of space for sauce. Just make sure you don't cut all the way through. Place 4 breasts in one casserole dish and 4 in the other, making sure one of the dishes is freezer-safe.

Preheat the oven to 425°F/220°C.

Put the tomato purée, onion granules, basil, oregano, salt, and black pepper into a bowl. Squeeze any excess moisture out of the capers and chop them roughly, then add them to the bowl along with the oil and hummus. Divide the mixture between the two casserole dishes, then get your hands in to encourage the mixture to get deep into those slits.

Cover one dish and pop it into the freezer. Place the other one in the oven and bake for 25 to 30 minutes.

Meanwhile prepare the couscous by grating the zucchini into a big bowl. Pour in the couscous, crush in the bouillon cube, then pour in boiling water until it reaches just ½ inch/1cm above the couscous line. Cover with plastic wrap and set aside.

Drain the chickpeas, then pop them into a small bowl and stir in the pesto and oil. Once all the water has been absorbed into the couscous, fluff it up with a fork, then add all the chickpeas and mix really well. By now the chicken should be ready.

Put half the couscous into a freezer bag and let cool before freezing.

Now it's time for lunch.

SERVES: 4 NOW AND 4 LATER   ACTIVE TIME: 15 MINUTES   TOTAL TIME: 45 MINUTES

I only recently discovered through the powers of social media that you can eat a kiwi with the skin on! I mean, why didn't I think of that? We eat peaches with their fuzzy skin and don't bat an eyelid, even if the sensation is that of licking a Russian Blue cat! Kiwis are a great balance of tart and sweet with the added pop of the little black crunchy seeds that make it much more than a lunchbox snack. This is a welcome change from a potato salad at a barbecue.

KIWI SALAD

5 tablespoons olive oil

5 tablespoons lemon juice

3 tablespoons honey

1 clove of garlic, finely grated

1 tablespoon za'atar

¼ cup tahini

1 red onion, peeled and finely diced

8 kiwis, firm but not overripe, ends trimmed, chopped into chunks, skins and all!

1 cucumber

7 oz feta, crumbled or roughly chopped

a small handful of fresh dill, finely chopped

2 tablespoons black sesame seeds

Start by making the dressing in the bottom of a large serving bowl. Saves on washing up if nothing else. Add the oil, lemon juice, honey, garlic, za'atar, and tahini and mix.

Now add the onion and mix really well. The onion will soften as it sits in the lemon juice. Now add the kiwi.

To prepare the cucumber, slice lengthwise and remove the seeds using a small spoon. Cut into long strips and then into cubes. Add to the bowl. Add the feta on top and sprinkle with the chopped dill and sesame seeds.

Don't mix the salad till you are ready to serve, or everything will wilt and go weird.

SERVES: 4–8   TOTAL TIME: 20 MINUTES

I discovered these in the frozen veg aisle and I have not looked back since. They are a great alternative to peas but firmer, less sweet, and simply delicious. So it's worth having a bag in the freezer, especially if you, like me, are not a huge pea fan … unless they're mushy.

EDAMAME WILD RICE SALAD

1⅓ cups cottage cheese

3-inch piece of ginger, peeled

½ teaspoon salt

¼ cup olive oil

2 tablespoons honey

1 lemon, juice and finely grated zest

1½ cups fresh parsley leaves

¼ cup pickled red cabbage

1¼ cups precooked wild rice (or precooked rice of your choice), cooled

4 cups frozen edamame beans, cooked and cooled

In a large serving bowl, add the cottage cheese and grate in the ginger.

Add the salt, oil, and honey, then the zest and juice of the lemon and mix really well.

Add the parsley leaves. I don't like chopping them up because I think parsley is so subtle it can almost be used as a leafy alternative in a salad. Keep the stalks, they would work well chopped into a chicken soup; freeze them in a bag, keeping the stalks whole.

Now add the pickled red cabbage and the rice. Add the cooled edamame beans and mix well.

SERVES: 4–8   TOTAL TIME: 15 MINUTES

Baked potatoes are my favorite lunch, simply with some beans and cheese. Or even just a knob of butter, seasoned well with some black pepper. But I like to make these when I have a little more time to spare. They are delicious and moist, with cottage cheese running through them, topped with sriracha and more cheese. I've also included some of my other favorite filling options on the next page if you fancy something different—or why not do a combination if there are a few of you?

COTTAGE CHEESE AND ONION POTATO SKINS

8 medium russet potatoes

1 small red onion, finely chopped

1 teaspoon garlic paste

1⅓ cups full-fat cottage cheese

½ teaspoon paprika

½ teaspoon salt, plus more for sprinkling

a few tablespoons oil

sriracha sauce, whichever is your favorite flavor

3½ oz red Leicester cheese or extra-sharp Cheddar cheese, freshly grated or frozen (I always have some in the freezer)

bunch of green onions, chopped, as optional garnish

Start by microwaving the potatoes. Prick them with a fork (so they don't explode), then lay them on their sides and microwave for 10 minutes. Turn them over and microwave again for another 10 minutes.

Meanwhile, put the red onion, garlic paste, cottage cheese, paprika, and salt into a bowl and give it a really good stir.

Preheat the oven to 425°F/220°C.

As soon as the potatoes are ready, put them onto 2 baking sheets, big enough to hold them all when they are cut in half. Drizzle them with oil and sprinkle generously with salt. This will give them a crisp skin. As soon as the potatoes are cool enough to handle, slice them in half lengthwise, then scoop out the flesh and put it into a bowl, being careful not to pierce the skins. Lay the skins back on the baking sheets, ready to fill.

Mash the potato flesh and mix in the cottage cheese mixture. Spoon this mixture back into the potato skins. Drizzle with the sriracha and sprinkle on the cheese. Bake in the oven for 20 minutes, until the cheese is bubbling and golden. Sprinkle with chopped green onions (if you like) and serve.

Any leftovers can be frozen uncovered until they are firm, then wrapped individually in foil.

SERVES: 8 (MAKES 16 HALVES)   ACTIVE TIME: 30 MINUTES   TOTAL TIME: 1 HOUR 15 MINUTES

POTATO SKINS FIVE WAYS

Here are some other filling variations for potato skins—the method is the same as on p. 90. Just mix the filling with the mashed potato, fill the skins, and top with cheese.

BACON + BEAN

1 x 15-oz can of baked beans + 1 teaspoon smoked paprika + ½ teaspoon salt + 4 bacon slices (turkey or vegetarian bacon works equally well), popped into a microwave for 1 minute, then thinly snipped with scissors + 2½ oz extra-sharp Cheddar cheese, grated, for the top

PESTO

3 tablespoons pesto + 7 oz feta cheese, crumbled + 2½ oz extra-sharp Cheddar cheese, grated, for the top

CHILI

1 x 15-oz can of chili con carne + 1 teaspoon chile flakes + 1 tablespoon Worcestershire sauce + ⅔ cup sour cream, mixed with 2½ oz extra-sharp Cheddar cheese, grated, for the top

BOMBAY MIX

3 tablespoons curry paste + 1 green chile, finely chopped + fresh cilantro, finely chopped + Bombay mix plus 2½ oz extra-sharp Cheddar cheese, grated, for the top

CORONATION TUNA

See p. 96

I grew up eating rice for every single meal, but I don't eat it as often now unless I'm at my mum's. But there is something so comforting about eating a lunch cooked in a big pot that really fills a gap. This rice dish is no exception. It's salty and sweet and perfect with prawns. Best of all, once you have made this pot for lunch, you have a second lot that can be frozen for dinner another day. I like to eat mine with a poached or fried egg—any situation where there is a runny warm egg adds to the deliciousness. Sprinkle some chopped red chile on top too, if you like.

PRAWN MALAY RICE

5 tablespoons vegetable oil

3 tablespoons garlic paste

2 small onions, chopped

1 teaspoon salt

5 tablespoons soy sauce

4 tablespoons honey

1 teaspoon chile powder

1 tablespoon curry powder

1½ quarts boiling water

3¾ cups basmati rice

11½ oz cooked king prawns or jumbo shrimp

1⅓ cups frozen peas

fried eggs (optional)

Put the oil into a large nonstick pan and turn the heat up to high. Add the garlic paste, followed quickly by the onions and salt. Give it a good stir to make sure that the onions don't burn too much, and keep them moving and browning.

Lower the heat completely, and add the soy sauce, honey, chile powder, and curry powder. Cook for 1 minute on medium heat.

Have the hot water at the ready. Add the rice to the pan and turn up the heat, stirring all the time. As you stir you will see the rice become white in the heat of the pan.

Now stir in the prawns. Pour in the water and keep stirring the rice on high heat. As soon as the liquid has thickened and the rice is more noticeable, add the peas, give it all a final stir, and pop the lid on. Turn the heat down to the lowest setting and let steam for at least 15 minutes.

Fluff the rice up with a spoon and let stand with the lid off for a few minutes before serving. Eat as is, or fry a few eggs while you wait for it to cool a little.

Freeze leftovers in a bag or tub once the rice is completely cool.

Coronation chicken sandwiches seemed a bizarre concept to me. I never found a halal one that I could try, but the color and the distinct lack of curryness made me suspicious. But I love how some things stand the test of time, and now this is one of my faves, and it works really well with tuna. With very little fishy flavor, it absorbs all the deliciousness of the Coronation flavors. I make enough of this so that I can make two sandwiches—one for me and one for the other half while we are on our lunch break. And I leave the rest of the tuna mix in the fridge for a salad or, better still, to top a hot baked potato, with some extra baby spinach.

CORONATION TUNA

3 x 5-oz cans of tuna chunks in water, drained

½ teaspoon ground cinnamon

1 teaspoon ground black pepper

1 heaped teaspoon curry powder, mild or hot, as you prefer

2 tablespoons mango chutney

2 tablespoons raisins

a pinch of salt

8–12 tablespoons full-fat mayonnaise

TO SERVE

4 slices of brown bread

butter, for spreading

baby spinach leaves

Put the tuna into a Tupperware container with a lid, making sure to drain off any excess moisture first. Nobody wants a soggy filling. (I'm mixing this in the Tupperware to save on washing up.) Add the cinnamon, black pepper, curry powder, mango chutney, raisins, and salt, and give it all a good mix until well combined.

Add the mayonnaise. I like a very creamy filling, so if you get to 8 spoons and think you have enough, that's totally up to you. I for one can keep going. Mix well.

Butter both slices of bread and layer on your tuna filling. Add the spinach and sandwich together.

Before you tuck in, close up your Tupperware and save the leftovers for another lunch during the week. You might like to use it as a filling for potato skins (see p. 92).

I cook the tortellini in the vegetable stock rather than boiling them separately—as the bits of filled pasta boil in the stock, they thicken the sauce, giving you a warming soup. And more than anything else, it saves on washing up. Everything that goes into this recipe uses up bits in jars and bits from the freezer, which means you can have a nice, wholesome warm lunch with as little prep as possible.

ONE-POT TORTELLINI

1 quart boiling water

2 vegetable stock cubes

1 teaspoon salt

½ teaspoon ground turmeric

1 teaspoon granulated garlic

1 teaspoon chile flakes

⅔ cup frozen peas

7 oz jarred asparagus, drained and roughly chopped

1 lb 5 oz filled tortellini

a large handful of fresh mint, chopped

1 lime, juice and finely grated zest

1 tablespoon unsalted butter

Bring the water to a boil in a saucepan on medium heat, then add the stock cubes and stir until dissolved. Add the salt, turmeric, garlic granules, chile flakes, and peas.

Add the chopped asparagus, along with the tortellini, and allow to gently boil for 5 minutes. Add the chopped mint and the lime juice and zest and take off the heat. Stir in the butter and let it melt. Then it's ready to eat.

As soon as it has cooled, if you want to, you can portion out into freezer- and microwave-safe containers with lids and freeze.

SERVES: 6 (SMALL PORTIONS)   TOTAL TIME: 15–20 MINUTES

Bread dipped in egg and fried is a winner any which way, and this is a little bit different from its sweet counterparts. I don't see why we can't have French toast for lunch instead of, or including, breakfast. It's great having these in the freezer, too, for those days when you don't have time to think about what to make for lunch. You can just pop them in the oven to reheat while you're getting on with other things.

SAVORY FRENCH TOAST

6 large eggs

7 tablespoons whole milk

½ teaspoon salt

2 teaspoons sugar

¼ teaspoon ground turmeric

1 teaspoon granulated garlic

1 teaspoon granulated onion

6 slices of white bread

3 slices of cooked ham/
  turkey/vegetarian ham

3 slices of mild cheese

vegetable oil, for frying

ketchup, to serve, optional

Put the eggs into a shallow bowl, wide enough to fit a slice of bread, and add the milk, salt, sugar, turmeric, garlic granules, and onion granules. Mix well and let sit for 5 minutes, allowing the granules to rehydrate in the egg mix.

Sandwich the slices of bread together with the ham and cheese. Dip them into the egg mixture and pop them on a plate.

Put a nonstick frying pan with a thin layer of oil in it on the stovetop. Take one of the sandwiches and dip it back into the egg mixture to get another soaking, then fry on medium heat for 3 minutes, until it has a golden color and the cheese begins to melt. Turn over and cook for another 3 minutes, pressing lightly with a spatula to help seal the bread, then pop the sandwich onto a plate lined with some paper towels.

Add some more oil to the pan and repeat with the other sandwiches, dipping and frying in the same way. Depending how absorbent the bread is, you may find you have enough eggy mix left to make another sandwich. When they're all done, cut the sandwiches in half.

Serve hot, with a dollop of ketchup if you like.

These are best eaten fresh, but if there are any left over, you can wrap them in foil and freeze them.

I don't know about you, but we always have baked beans in the cupboard, so this is a great recipe for if you want to try something different with them. It might sound unusual . . . you're just going to have to trust me on this one! If you also like coleslaw, double up the sauce ingredients in **bold** and pop the extra ingredients on your shopping list.

BAKED BEAN FALAFEL

FOR THE FALAFEL

4 x 15-oz/400g cans of baked beans

1 large egg

6 cloves of garlic, crushed

1 large onion, chopped

1 teaspoon salt

1 teaspoon chile powder

1 tablespoon ground cumin

1 tablespoon ground coriander

1⅓ cups/120g chickpea flour

cooking oil spray

FOR THE SAUCE

1 clove of garlic, grated

1 teaspoon salt

¼ cup/55g mayonnaise

a squeeze of lemon juice

1 tablespoon chopped fresh parsley

2 tablespoons sriracha sauce

COLESLAW (OPTIONAL)

3 carrots, grated

½ white cabbage, shredded

½ red cabbage, shredded

1 red onion, thinly sliced

Drain the beans, keeping the liquid aside in a separate bowl, then rinse the beans and let them drain. Put the beans and the egg into a blender and whiz until you have a smooth paste. Transfer to a bowl and add the garlic, onion, salt, chile powder, cumin, and coriander. Add the chickpea flour and mix everything together—it may be quite a wet mix.

Preheat the oven to 425°F/220°C and have a large baking sheet ready, generously greased.

Using wet hands, create walnut-sized balls of the bean mixture and pop them on the sheet. Spray them with oil all over and bake in the oven for 25 to 30 minutes, turning them halfway through.

To make the sauce, add the garlic, salt, mayonnaise, lemon juice, parsley, and sriracha to ½ cup plus 2 tablespoons/150ml of the reserved bean liquid from the cans. Stir and set aside.

If you don't want to waste the rest of the bean juice, double up the sauce ingredients to make a double batch. Use half as a dipping sauce for the falafel. Stir the other half into the coleslaw ingredients listed.

When the falafel are baked, I like to eat them squashed inside a soft bun, smothered with the sauce and some salad (and some of the coleslaw, if I've made it). There is plenty here to eat and to freeze, so pop the extras into a freezer bag.

The coleslaw will keep in the fridge for 2 to 3 days. Serve alongside cold cuts or in a baked potato.

MAKES: 20–24   ACTIVE TIME: 30 MINUTES   TOTAL TIME: 1 HOUR

Make a coleslaw at the same time as the Baked Bean Falafels (see p. 100) and you have the perfect accompaniment for many other dishes.

I didn't grow up eating cheese or with it being around the house. It's very not Bengali of me when I pick cheese and crackers over a curry, but there you go. This Indian cheese is like halloumi, creamy yet it doesn't melt. It's great for absorbing flavors and takes on the deliciousness of anything you put with it. Best of all it can be frozen, so it means I have spicy cheese on tap. I am making enough filling here for six pockets, with some left over to either freeze or add to pasta to make a delicious pasta salad. When you have double quantities, you have done the hard work once and you can decide later how to eat it, again!

PANEER PITA

¼ cup vegetable oil,
  plus a dash

2 x 9-oz packs of paneer,
  cubed

2 tablespoons garlic paste

1 large red onion, sliced

1 teaspoon salt

1 tablespoon tomato paste

2 large red bell peppers,
  thinly sliced

1 teaspoon ground cumin

1 teaspoon chile flakes

1 tablespoon honey

1 lemon, juice and finely
  grated zest

fresh cilantro, chopped

4 cups watercress or arugula,
  roughly chopped

3 pita breads

Start by putting the oil into a nonstick frying pan on high heat. Add the cubes of paneer and fry, making sure to stir occasionally so that the cheese turns golden brown—not only does this add to the flavor, but it also creates a texture that the sauce can adhere to. Fry for about 5 minutes, then transfer to a plate.

Add another small dash of oil and lower the heat to medium. Add the garlic paste and cook for 1 minute, then add the sliced red onions and salt and cook for a few minutes, until the onions are soft.

Squeeze in the tomato paste and cook for 1 minute. Add a few splashes of cold water to prevent it from sticking. Throw in the peppers, cumin, and chile flakes and cook for another 10 minutes with the lid on, until the peppers are soft and limp.

Pour in the honey, then add the lemon juice and zest and the paneer and cook on high heat for 2 to 3 minutes. The mixture should be dry and the cubes of cheese should be coated with the sauce.

Take off the heat, then stir in the cilantro and watercress—the cress does not need cooking, it will wilt from the heat of everything else surrounding it yet maintain some of its fire.

Halve the pita breads and toast them, then fill with the mixture.

Pop the filling you have left over into a Tupperware container and, when it is totally cool, freeze it or stick it in the fridge for later (or see opposite for how to make a pasta salad out of it).

SERVES: 6 NOT SO HUNGRY,
3 VERY HUNGRY

ACTIVE TIME: 10 MINUTES   TOTAL TIME: 20 MINUTES

PANEER PASTA SALAD

This is a great way of using up any leftovers you have of that tasty cheese without having to serve it exactly the same way. Mix 10½ oz of cooked and cooled pasta with the leftover paneer. Add ½ a chopped cucumber and a small bag of watercress or arugula. Stir in a few tablespoons of yogurt, mix well, and you have a really simple pasta salad.

Chow mein is the easiest thing to order, but even easier to make. I love the flavors of honey mustard, so I'm keeping it simple. I also whip up a double batch and skewer half the chicken for the freezer, so if I have to make a quick lunch or need something to whack on a grill, I have the same honey mustard chicken, minus the chow mein. If you don't want the extra in the freezer, simply halve the ingredients in **bold**.

HONEY MUSTARD CHOW MEIN

10 boneless, skinless chicken thighs, thinly sliced

¼ cup honey

¼ cup whole-grain mustard

4 cloves of garlic, minced

1-inch piece of ginger, peeled and grated

¼ cup soy sauce

1 teaspoon salt

3 tablespoons sriracha sauce

vegetable oil, for frying

2 medium onions, thinly sliced

1 lb stir-fry vegetables

10 oz cooked noodles

a large handful of fresh cilantro

⅓ cup salted peanuts, roughly chopped

wedges of lime

Put the chicken thighs into a large bowl with the honey, mustard, garlic, ginger, soy sauce, salt, and sriracha and let marinate.

Place a large nonstick frying pan or wok on the stovetop on high heat. Add some oil and, when it's really hot, add the onions. When they are very brown, add half the marinated chicken, putting the other half into the fridge for later.

Continue cooking the chicken on high heat, and when it is cooked through, add the stir-fry veg and the noodles and mix together before lowering to medium heat for 5 minutes, or until the vegetables are just a little bit soft but still crisp.

Take off the heat, sprinkle with the cilantro and peanuts, and serve with a wedge of lime—and I'm always tempted to add another dash of sriracha.

Once you have eaten, see the box below for storage and prep instructions for the reserved marinated chicken in the fridge.

CHICKEN SKEWERS

If you have made a double batch of chicken, put half of the marinated meat onto skewers and pop on a baking sheet to freeze. When frozen, take the skewers off the sheet and put them into a freezer bag to store.

Defrost fully when needed, then cook in a preheated oven (425°F/ 220°C) for 30 minutes, turning halfway through.

SERVES: 4   TOTAL TIME: 40 MINUTES

As the kids get bigger, they seem to get busier, with social calendars that make my schedule look as bare as my cupboards on a Saturday evening before a weekly shop. So this is just another really easy way to make a hot sandwich that is transportable, warm, and yummy. One of these days I will be partying as much as my kids—not any time soon though.

CORNED BEEF SUB

3 tablespoons vegetable oil

2 cloves of garlic, crushed

1 large onion, diced

½ teaspoon salt

1 red bell pepper, diced

2 medium potatoes, peeled and diced into ½-inch pieces

½ teaspoon ground turmeric

½ teaspoon chile powder

1 lemon, finely grated zest and juice

2 x 12-oz cans of corned beef, diced into ½-inch pieces

4 sub rolls

5¼ oz Gouda cheese, grated

TO SERVE

sriracha sauce

arugula or lettuce

Heat the oil in a large nonstick frying pan, then add the garlic and onion and cook for a few minutes, until soft and translucent. Add the salt and cook until the onions are golden brown.

Add the red bell pepper and potatoes and cook with a lid on for 10 minutes. If it starts to stick, add a small splash of water to create some steam for the potatoes to cook.

Now mix in the turmeric, chile powder, and lemon zest and juice. Stir in the corned beef and continue to cook on medium heat.

Preheat the oven to 375°F/200°C.

As soon as the potatoes are tender, take the pan off the heat. Lay the four sub rolls, sliced and open, on a baking sheet and fill one half of each with the corned beef mixture in an even layer. Sprinkle with the cheese and bake in the oven until it has melted.

Take out and drizzle with sriracha, then fill with arugula or lettuce and close the rolls up.

If you have any filling left over, it can be frozen, then thawed and used again in the same way. Or, for a traditional corned beef hash breakfast, add a couple of dashes of Worcestershire sauce when reheating, stir in some chopped parsley, and serve with a fried egg on top.

SERVES: 4   ACTIVE TIME: 15 MINUTES   TOTAL TIME: 40 MINUTES

These cloud breads are so light it's like eating air, but delicious air. I like making them but I also like topping them—they are great carriers of strong flavors. Without the topping, the breads can be used as carb-free pizza bases or burger buns, or can be toasted and eaten with butter and jam. The fish mix also makes a great filling for an omelet—or a showstopping tart.

CLOUD BREAD WITH CREAMY MACKEREL TOPPING

FOR THE BREAD

cooking oil spray

4 large eggs, separated

1¾ oz/50g full-fat cream cheese

¼ teaspoon cream of tartar

FOR THE TOPPING

3½ oz/100g cream cheese

3 tablespoons whole milk

1 teaspoon nigella seeds or any black seeds (such as black sesame seeds, brown mustard seeds, or even poppy seeds)

2 green onions, finely chopped

a squeeze of lemon juice

salt, to taste

9 oz/250g hot smoked mackerel fillets, flaked

Preheat the oven to 300°F/150°C. Grease and line two baking sheets with parchment paper.

Whisk the egg whites to stiff peaks. Using the same whisk, in a different bowl whisk the yolks with the cream cheese and cream of tartar. Add the whisked egg whites a little at a time until the mixture is well incorporated. There will be lumps, but that is normal.

Take large spoonfuls of the mixture and make 4 or 5 rounds on one of the baking sheets, making sure the rounds are not touching. Bake the first batch in the oven for 20 minutes. While that's happening, make the topping by mixing the cream cheese with the milk, nigella seeds, green onions, lemon juice, and a sprinkle of salt. Stir in the flaked mackerel.

As soon as the first batch of bread comes out of the oven, they are ready to be lightly topped with the creamy fish mixture. Take them off the sheet and let cool completely.

Make the rest of the cloud bread in the same way. If the remaining mixture separates while the first batch is baking, just give it a stir to bring it back together.

CREAMY MACKEREL TART

You can add 2 large eggs and 3 tablespoons of heavy cream to the fish mix and use it as a tart filling. Line a 7-inch/18cm tart pan with 10½ oz/300g of store-bought shortcrust pastry, then add a sheet of parchment paper and some baking weights. Bake in the oven at 350°F/180°C for 20 minutes, then remove the weights and bake for another 5 minutes. Spoon in the filling, then lower the oven temperature to 325°F/160°C and bake for another 25 minutes.

MAKES: 8–10   ACTIVE TIME: 20 MINUTES   TOTAL TIME: 1 HOUR

I love a tart—they are simple to make, feel impressive, and have endless flavor possibilities. The filling for this is so good that I've come up with some other ways you can use it. Double the ingredients in **bold** if you want to make a curry or a soup at the same time—see opposite.

SWEET POTATO AND GOAT CHEESE TART

FOR THE PASTRY

2 cups plus
6 tablespoons/300g
all-purpose flour, plus
more for dusting

a pinch of salt

½ cup plus 2 tablespoons
/150g cold unsalted
butter, cubed

3 to 4 tablespoons
cold water

FOR THE FILLING

**2 tablespoons
vegetable oil**

**2 cloves of garlic,
crushed**

**1 large sprig of fresh
thyme**

**1 medium red onion,
sliced**

½ teaspoon salt

**1 large sweet potato,
peeled and cut into
½-inch/1cm cubes
(about 10 ½ oz/300g)**

3½ oz/100g goat
cheese

3 large eggs

¾ cup plus
1 tablespoon/200g
crème fraîche

½ teaspoon salt

1 teaspoon paprika

Start by making the pastry. Put the flour and salt into a bowl, then add the butter and rub it into the flour until it resembles breadcrumbs. Add 1 tablespoon of water at a time until the dough comes together.

Dust a work surface with flour and roll out the pastry until it is large enough to cover the bottom and sides of a deep 9-inch/23cm tart pan with a removable bottom and leave a ½-inch/1cm overhang. Prick the dough a few times, then pop the tart shell into the freezer for 15 minutes. Preheat the oven to 400°F/200°C.

Now make the filling. Heat the oil in a pan with a lid, then add the garlic and cook until golden—this should only take a few minutes. Add the thyme sprig, along with the onion and salt, and cook until the onions are soft. Stir in the sweet potatoes, then pop the pan on low to medium heat and cover to allow the potatoes to soften. This should take about 10 minutes.

Take the tart shell out of the freezer. Put a piece of parchment paper inside, with some baking weights, and bake in the oven for 15 minutes.

The sweet potatoes should be cooked by now, so take them off the heat and let cool a little. Discard the thyme sprig, but leave the little leaves in there.

Make the dressing by whizzing together the watercress, lemon zest and juice, pine nuts, oil, and salt in a blender.

Take the tart shell out of the oven, remove the paper and weights, and bake for another 5 minutes. Take it out, and lower the oven temperature to 350°F/180°C.

Spoon the potato mixture into the tart shell and scatter the chunks of goat cheese all over.

FOR THE DRESSING

4 cups/85g watercress

1 lemon, finely grated zest
   and juice

¾ cup/100g pine nuts

5 tablespoons/75ml olive oil

a pinch of salt

Put the eggs, crème fraîche, salt, and paprika into a bowl and mix until well combined. Pour into the tart shell, dot a few small spoonfuls of the dressing over the top, and bake in the oven for 30 to 35 minutes.

Use the rest of the dressing to dress a simple green salad mixed with tomatoes, or as a dressing for Hasselback Squash (see p. 180).

Allow the tart to cool in the pan for 10 minutes, then trim the edges. Let it cool in the pan for another 30 minutes before taking it out. Serve the tart warm or chilled.

Any leftovers can be kept in the fridge for 3 days or frozen.

SWEET POTATO AND GOAT CHEESE CURRY

You can also make a great curry by adding a few extra ingredients. Add a large glug of vegetable oil to a large pot and heat over medium heat. Add two red onions, chopped into large chunks. As soon as the onions are soft, add 4 generous tablespoons of curry paste (see p. 240) and heat through. Add two large sweet potatoes (peeled and diced) to the pan and give everything a good mix. Add 2 cups hot water and let simmer over low to medium heat, with the lid on, for 25 minutes, making sure to check and stir occasionally. As soon as the potatoes are tender, take off the heat and stir in some chopped watercress. Sprinkle with some pine nuts and serve with a dollop of yogurt and some naan on the side.

SWEET POTATO AND GOAT CHEESE SOUP

The filling works great as a soup, and for that I double the first 7 filling ingredients and blend them with 2 cups of vegetable stock. This makes 4 servings and can be frozen or stored in the fridge for 3 days. Garnish with your choice of herbs—I use thyme, watercress—some paprika, and a splash of olive oil. You can also add some of the leftover dressing, extra pine nuts, and a crumbling of goat cheese.

The filling for the Goat Cheese Tart works great as both a soup
and as the base of a curry. By adding a few extra ingredients
you have two delicious alternatives, perfect if friends pop around,
or to store away in the freezer.

Fish burgers are our favorite thing to eat—they're warming and comforting. Imagine all your favorite foods in burger form! Well, that's a challenge if ever I heard one. These fish pie patties are all nuzzled inside a soft white bun squished with a pea tartare! Yum. I tend to make my own bread for this recipe, but there's nothing wrong with store-bought if you need to save a little time. I like to serve them with oven fries alongside.

FISH PIE BURGERS

FOR THE FISH PIE PATTIES

1½ lb russet potatoes, peeled and diced

3 large eggs

2 x 12-oz packages of fish pie mix

1¼ cups water

2 cloves of garlic, grated

1 lemon, finely grated zest only (keep juice for the pea tartare)

1 teaspoon salt

1 teaspoon onion salt

1 teaspoon ground black pepper

a small handful of fresh parsley, finely chopped

½ a bunch of fresh chives, chopped

vegetable oil, for frying

Put the potatoes into a pot of cold water and bring to a boil, putting the eggs into the pot at the same time. Boil until the potatoes are tender when poked with a fork. Drain, then tip the potatoes into a large bowl and leave the colander in the sink for the fish.

Peel the eggs. Mash the potatoes and let cool (I open a window so that the breeze cools them in no time). Grate the eggs straight into the bowl of potatoes.

Pop the fish into a pan with the water, bring to a boil, then let simmer for just 5 minutes. Drain the fish in the same colander you used for the potatoes. Once the fish is cool enough to handle, flake it into the bowl of egg and potato.

To shape the fish patties, have a large baking sheet ready. Add the garlic, lemon zest, salt, onion salt, pepper, parsley, and chives to the bowl of fish and potato, then get your hands in and give it a good mix. Divide the mixture into 8 portions and shape into patties (you may need to wet your hands to make sure it doesn't all stick to your fingers). Place on the sheet and pop into the fridge while you prepare the pea tartare.

SERVES: 8   ACTIVE TIME: 30 MINUTES   TOTAL TIME: 45 MINUTES

FOR THE PEA TARTARE

1⅓ cups frozen peas

5 heaped tablespoons
  mayonnaise

1 teaspoon mustard powder

1 small onion, finely chopped

a squeeze of lemon juice

a small handful of fresh
  parsley, chopped

a sprinkling of salt

FOR THE COATING

1⅔ cups all-purpose flour

3 large eggs, beaten

1⅔ cups plain breadcrumbs

8 white burger buns
  (see p. 244 if you'd like
  to make your own)

Put the peas into a bowl of boiling water and set aside for a few minutes to defrost, then drain them and pop them into a bowl. Using the back of a fork, just mush them lightly. Stir in the mayo, mustard, onion, lemon juice, parsley, and salt and set aside.

Put the flour, beaten egg, and breadcrumbs in separate shallow dishes. Take the fish patties out of the fridge and dip each one first into the flour, then into the egg, then into the breadcrumbs and put them back on the sheet.

If you are making oven fries to go with the fish pie burgers, now's the time to get them in.

Place a medium-size nonstick frying pan on medium heat and add ½ inch of oil. Have a baking sheet lined with paper towels ready. Fry 2 patties at a time, for 2 minutes on each side. Once they are fried, pop them onto the prepared sheet while you finish frying the rest.

To make up your burgers, slice the buns across the middle. Add a patty to each one, then a spoonful of the pea tartare, and put the tops of the buns back on.

If you are only eating a few burgers and want to save some, they can be cooled, wrapped in foil minus the pea tartare, and frozen.

I've seen these poke bowls popping up all over the place, especially when I'm in and around London. I've seen a few at festivals too—it's like they're trying to say, "Make way, sushi." These have all the deliciousness of sushi but in a bowl, which means there is more of it. With a sticky rice base, they can be topped with fresh ingredients, or leftovers from the fridge—make it colorful, make it delicious, make it yours. The sauce also makes a great marinade for chicken wings—double the ingredients in **bold** and see below for how to use it.

BLACK PEPPER POKE SALMON BOWLS

FOR THE RICE

2½ cups sushi rice/sticky rice

2 tablespoons apple cider vinegar

1 teaspoon salt

2 teaspoons sugar

FOR THE SAUCE

2 tablespoons mayonnaise

1 tablespoon soy sauce

1 teaspoon sesame oil

½ teaspoon fish sauce

1 tablespoon sriracha sauce

1 lemon, juice only

1 teaspoon ground black pepper

TO FINISH

2 really fresh skinless salmon fillets (7 oz each), cubed

2 small or 1 large avocado, sliced (with a squeeze of lemon to prevent browning)

¼ cup pickled red cabbage

1 large carrot, peeled and grated

a large handful of salted peanuts, roughly chopped

2 green onions, sliced

sesame seeds

nori sheets, snipped into strips

ground black pepper

Start with the rice: Place it in a saucepan and rinse it until the water runs clear. Add just enough water to come ½ inch above the rice. Stirring all the time, place on high heat (stirring will ensure that the rice doesn't settle on the bottom). Once it comes to a boil, let it simmer on medium heat until all the water has evaporated. Pop the lid on and leave on the lowest setting to steam about 10 minutes.

Meanwhile, gather together everything you need to finish off this bowl.

Make the sauce by mixing together the mayo, soy sauce, sesame oil, fish sauce, sriracha, lemon juice, and black pepper. Put the salmon into a bowl, then pour in the sauce (half if you're making chicken wings as well) and mix thoroughly.

Once the rice has steamed, mix the vinegar, salt, and sugar in a small bowl, then pour over the rice and stir well.

Divide the rice among four bowls and start adding all the different finishing ingredients. The salmon first, then the avocado, red cabbage, carrot, and peanuts. Sprinkle with the green onions, sesame, and nori, add a sprinkling of black pepper, and you're ready to eat.

MARINATED CHICKEN WINGS

Pour the remaining half of the sauce over 2 lb 2 oz chicken wings and mix well to coat. Pop the wings into a freezer bag and freeze for another day. To use, defrost fully and bake at 425°F/220°C for 40 minutes, turning halfway through.

SERVES: 4

ACTIVE TIME: 30 MINUTES   TOTAL TIME: 45 MINUTES

Does "pie plate" mean it's my plate and all the pie is mine too? This pie is covered in butter pastry and filled with Bombay-style potatoes and corned beef. Not something I was used to eating, but I'm happy to admit I love the stuff now! I always make two of these, one to eat and one to freeze, so double up all the ingredients if you fancy doing that. You can also prepare this in advance and cook it from frozen if you want to save even more time.

CORNED BEEF BOMBAY PIE

FOR THE PASTRY

3⅔ cups/450g all-purpose flour, plus extra for dusting

a pinch of salt

¾ cup plus 2 tablespoons/200g unsalted butter, cubed

a few tablespoons of cold water

1 egg, beaten

FOR THE FILLING

2 tablespoons vegetable oil

1 teaspoon Bengali Spice Mix (Panch Phoran—see p. 237)

3 cloves of garlic, crushed

1 medium onion, finely chopped

1 celery stalk, finely diced

1 teaspoon salt

½ teaspoon ground turmeric

1 teaspoon paprika

1 large potato, peeled and cut into 1-inch/2.5cm cubes

1 carrot, peeled and sliced into ¼-inch/5mm coins

1 small red bell pepper, cut into ½-inch/1cm dice

7 tablespoons/100ml water

1 tablespoon tamarind paste

12 oz/340g corned beef, cut into 1-inch/2.5cm cubes

a small handful of fresh cilantro, roughly chopped

Start with the pastry. Put the flour into a bowl with the salt and rub in the butter until it resembles breadcrumbs. Add the water a little at a time to bring the dough together, and as soon as you have done that, cut off one third of the dough. Wrap both pieces and put into the fridge to chill.

Now to the filling. Put the oil into a medium nonstick pan and add the spice mix. As soon as the seeds start to pop, add the garlic, onion, celery, and salt. Cook on high heat until the onions are soft, then lower the heat, add the turmeric and paprika, and cook for 1 minute. Add the potatoes, carrots, red bell pepper, water, and tamarind and cook for about 20 minutes on medium heat with the lid on, until the potatoes are cooked. Take off the lid to dry out any extra moisture. Take off the heat, stir in the corned beef and cilantro, then transfer to a plate to cool.

Preheat the oven to 425°F/220°C and place a baking sheet in it.

Roll out the larger bit of pastry to the thickness of a coin (about ⅛ inch/3mm) and big enough to cover the bottom and sides of a 9-inch/23cm ovenproof pie plate and leave a slight overhang. I like to use an enamel plate. Roll out the other piece so it fits the top with a small overhang. Spoon the filling over the pastry in the plate, then brush the edges with beaten egg and top with the smaller piece of pastry. Cut off the overhang, crimp the edges, and brush the top with egg. Cut a slit in the top and bake for 30 to 35 minutes.

When it's ready, allow it to rest for 20 minutes before eating.

If you are preparing this in advance, to be baked at a later date, do everything but the egg wash and place in the freezer. Preheat the oven to 400°F/200°C, brush your egg wash over the frozen pastry, then bake from frozen for 45 to 50 minutes, until piping hot all the way through.

SERVES: 4–6

ACTIVE TIME: 40 MINUTES   TOTAL TIME: 2 HOURS

A kedgeree to me is a mash-up of flavors in a staple such as rice, topped off with some eggs. I used to have this all the time as a child, because we always had leftover rice. But why not mix things up? The big bold colors in this just make me want to eat it with my eyes before any other sense. You will probably have enough here to freeze some for another day, too.

WATERCRESS QUINOA KEDGEREE

1¾ cups quinoa

3 tablespoons vegetable stock or water

6 cloves of garlic, peeled

2 x 3-oz bags of watercress

1¼ cups fresh cilantro

scant 1 oz fresh chives

1 tablespoon salt

4 tablespoons vegetable oil

1 large onion, thinly sliced

¼ cup butter

2 tablespoons Bengali Spice Mix (Panch Phoran—see p. 237)

1 quart water

2 large red chiles, sliced

8½ oz smoked trout, flaked

6 hard-boiled eggs

paprika, to serve

Start by rinsing the quinoa and setting it aside to drain. Put the stock into a blender with the garlic, watercress, cilantro, chives, salt, and 2 tablespoons of oil and blend to a smooth paste.

Heat the other 2 tablespoons of oil in a medium nonstick pan on high heat. Add the onion and cook, stirring occasionally until it turns a dark brown. As soon as it does, turn the heat down and add the butter and Bengali spice mix—when the spices start to pop, add the rinsed quinoa and the water and bring to a boil, stirring all the time. Then lower the heat and let simmer until all the liquid has evaporated. Take off the heat and stir in the watercress mixture, sliced chiles, and smoked trout flakes.

To serve, dish up the kedgeree and serve with the quartered eggs and a sprinkling of paprika. Any leftovers can be cooled and frozen (remove any hard-boiled eggs from these portions as they'll go rubbery when frozen).

SERVES: 4   ACTIVE TIME: 30 MINUTES   TOTAL TIME: 1 HOUR

We never really ate flatbreads or chapatis when I was growing up, so I didn't know how to make them until my husband expressed a keen interest when we got married and told me his maximum was 14 in one sitting. That is incentive enough to make these delicious flatbreads. They look like parathas but taste like pizza, and they're even better with a garlic and herb dip on the side.

PIZZA PARATHAS

FOR THE PARATHAS

4¾ cups/600g all-purpose flour, plus extra for dusting

2 teaspoons salt

2 teaspoons sugar

½ cup/120ml vegetable oil

1¼ cups/300ml boiling water

½ cup plus 2 tablespoons/ 150g unsalted butter

FOR THE PIZZA FILLING

⅓ cup/80g tomato paste

1 tablespoon dried oregano

6 tablespoons/40g grated hard cheese (such as red Leicester, sharp Cheddar, or Parmesan)

1 clove of garlic, grated

FOR THE DIP

3½ oz/100g cream cheese

3 tablespoons yogurt

1 clove of garlic, grated

a small handful of fresh chives, finely chopped

a squeeze of lemon

a pinch of salt and pepper

Put the flour, salt, and sugar into a bowl and stir in the oil. Make a well in the center and add the boiling water. Using a splatula, because the water is still very hot, roughly bring the dough together.

Drop the mixture onto a work surface and knead until you have a smooth dough. This should take a few minutes. Pop it into the bowl again and let rest, covered.

Meanwhile, you can make the filling and dip. To make the filling, put the tomato paste, oregano, cheese, and garlic into a bowl and give it a mix. To make the dip, put the cream cheese, yogurt, garlic, chives, lemon, and salt and pepper into another bowl, mix, and place in the fridge.

Roll the dough out into a long sausage shape and cut it into 12 equal portions. Roll each one into a ball and set them in a pile on the side. Take one ball and roll it out to a circle as thin as you can get it—you should be able to see the work surface through the dough in places.

Take 1 teaspoon of the tomato mixture, which should be like a paste, and spread it lightly all over the dough. Roll the dough up like a jelly roll, making sure to pinch and stretch it at the ends as you go along. Set aside and repeat with the rest of the balls of dough.

Take each dough sausage and roll inward to create what looks like a cinnamon roll, tucking the end into the base. Melt the butter and have a pastry brush at the ready. Now lightly flour the work surface and roll each paratha out into a thin circle just under ⅛-inch/3mm thick.

Pop a nonstick pan on medium to low heat. Place one paratha at a time in the pan and cook gently for 2 to 3 minutes on each side. Brush both sides with melted butter and transfer to a plate, with a piece of foil over the top to keep them warm while you make the rest. Serve straight away with the dip, as a light lunch.

These parathas are best frozen uncooked, layered with parchment paper in between so they don't stick.

MAKES: 12   TOTAL TIME: 1 HOUR

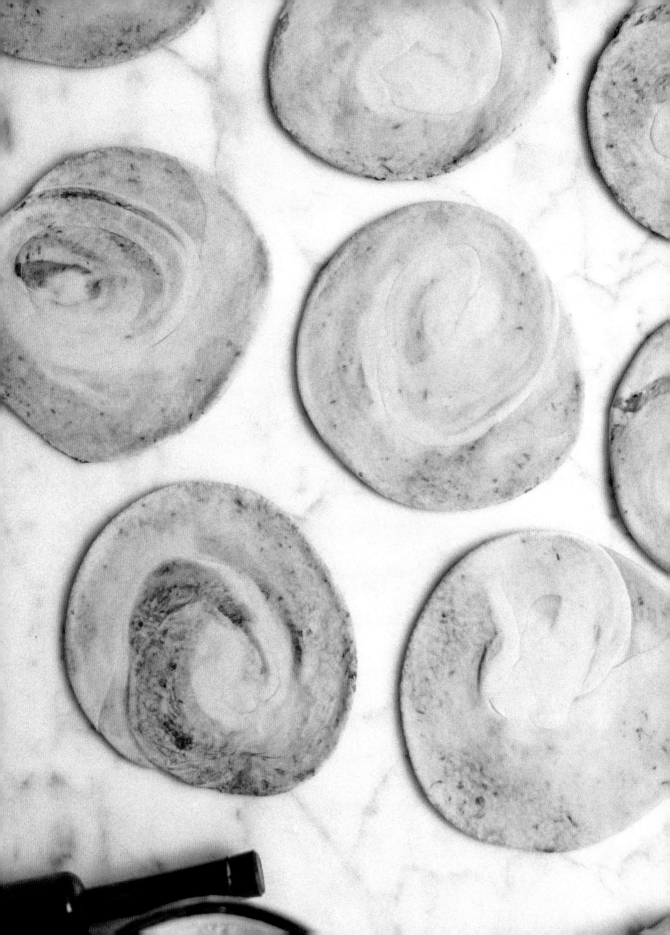

These are delicious cooked and served immediately, but if
you have more than you need, they freeze perfectly with a sheet
of parchment paper placed between each paratha. They will
freeze for up to 6 months.

DINNER

A good teriyaki is made even more delicious when the fish marinates in the sauce overnight in the fridge, but there is nothing to say that it can't be instant. It can, and it should be. We can have delicious food and eat it straight away. Best of all, you can make this, have your dinner, and put some fillets into the freezer for another day. And while the fish cooks, you can mix up a quick mango salsa to go with it.

TERIYAKI SALMON WITH MANGO SALSA

FOR THE TERIYAKI SALMON

½ cup plus 2 tablespoons water

1 teaspoon cornstarch

¼ cup soy sauce

¼ cup honey

1 tablespoon fish sauce

½ tablespoon ground ginger

½ tablespoon granulated garlic

½ tablespoon chile flakes

4 salmon fillets

9 oz precooked basmati rice (in a microwaveable package)

2 tablespoons vegetable oil, for frying

white sesame seeds (optional)

FOR THE SALSA

1 lb 2 oz mango chunks or a 15-oz can of mango, drained

1 lime, finely grated zest and juice

1 tablespoon dried cilantro or a small handful of fresh cilantro, chopped

1 red chile, frozen or fresh

Start by making the teriyaki sauce. Put the water into a bowl with the cornstarch and stir until the water is cloudy. Now add the soy sauce, honey, fish sauce, ginger, garlic granules, and chile flakes, and stir. Add the salmon fillets and let them marinate while you make the mango salsa.

Chop the mango into bite-size pieces and put into a bowl. Mix in the zest and juice of the lime and the cilantro. If you are using fresh chile, chop it finely and stir it in, or, if you have some frozen red chiles in the freezer, simply grate one in and mix.

Now cook the rice in the microwave per the package instructions.

Place a nonstick frying pan (ideally one with a lid, but a sheet of foil will do) on medium to high heat and add the oil. Add 2 salmon fillets, along with half the teriyaki marinade. Leave the rest in the bowl for now.

Cook for 2 minutes on one side, depending on the thickness of the fillet, then flip over and cook for 2 minutes on the other. Make sure that, with all the honey in the sauce, it isn't sticking or getting too thick—if it is, just turn the heat down and give the sauce a stir. Turn the heat off and cover with a lid or a piece of foil. The trapped heat will steam the thickest part of the fillet.

Before serving, put the remaining marinade and the other 2 fillets into a freezer bag and stick it in the freezer, ready for the next time you want teriyaki. Serve up the rice alongside the mango salsa, top with the rest of the salmon, drizzle with the sauce, and finish with a small sprinkling of sesame seeds.

Sometimes I want to eat something light and quick, and soup does not have to be laborious or long-winded. And even when you're doing quick and easy you can plan for the week ahead. This recipe uses bits out of jars that, when put together, can make something altogether delicious. And while you're making the soup, you can be baking some spicy seeds to go on top and to snack on later.

THAI RED PEPPER SOUP

FOR THE SOUP

¼ cup vegetable oil

1 tablespoon garlic paste

4 teaspoons Thai red curry paste

1 teaspoon salt

1 x 17-oz jar of roasted red peppers, drained

1 tablespoon dried cilantro

1½ quarts boiling water

2 slices of bread, stale or fresh, the middle or the thick end

1 cup coconut milk

FOR THE SPICY SEEDS

1 large egg white

3¼ cups sunflower seeds

½ teaspoon salt

½ teaspoon sugar

1 teaspoon paprika

1 teaspoon granulated garlic

½ cup dried shredded coconut

1 teaspoon dried cilantro

Start by making the soup. This is almost an all-in-one, whack-the-lid-on kind of job, but you will notice I said almost—everything benefits from cooking out, especially the Thai red curry paste.

First, preheat the oven to 350°F/180°C, ready for making the spicy seeds later.

Put the oil into a large saucepan and bring the heat up to medium. Add the garlic paste, red curry paste, and salt and cook the paste out. If it starts to stick, turn the heat down and add a splash of water to prevent it from burning.

Meanwhile, roughly chop the roasted red peppers and add them and the dried cilantro to the curry paste mixture. Pour in the boiling water—this helps to speed up the process. Tear in chunks of the bread and bring back to a boil, then cook it at a rapid simmer.

Now make your spicy seeds. Whisk the egg white in a bowl until foamy. Stir in the sunflower seeds, making sure all of them have an even coating. Sprinkle in the salt, sugar, paprika, and garlic granules and mix well, without using your spoon (otherwise all the flavor will stick to it!).

Toss in the coconut and cilantro, then spread the seeds on a baking sheet in an even layer. Bake in the oven for 10 to 12 minutes, but be sure to keep an eye on them—they will need turning halfway through. Once the seeds are dry to the touch, they are ready to go. Take them out of the oven and set aside.

Meanwhile, add the coconut milk to the pan of soup, stir well, then whiz until smooth, using an immersion blender.

To serve, ladle the soup into bowls and sprinkle with some of those delicious spicy sunflower seeds and a drizzle of oil, if you like. There will be plenty of soup to freeze, and the best way to do this is in individual portions. As for the seeds, you will have plenty of those to sprinkle on whatever you like or just for snacking. Store them in a clean jar.

SERVES: 4 PLUS MORE FOR ANOTHER DAY

TOTAL TIME: 30 MINUTES

I don't always like having a sit-down dinner. I quite like simple things that can be eaten while watching TV. I'm pretty sure that's the same for most of us. Busy lives sometimes mean quick dinners. This is really easy to make—it's sweet with a hint of spice, and, best of all, I always make plenty to store in the fridge or freezer for another day. It uses canned cod roe, something I don't think we use often enough.

COD ROE PÂTÉ

3 tablespoons vegetable oil

½ cup plus 2 tablespoons butter (salted or unsalted, whatever you have)

2 medium onions, chopped

1 teaspoon sugar

3 x 7-oz cans of pressed cod roe, cut into small cubes

1 teaspoon chile powder

2 teaspoons curry powder

1 teaspoon garam masala

½ cup plus 2 tablespoons heavy cream

TO EAT

crispbread or crackers or a plate of toast

eggplant pickle (that's the one I like to eat it with), or a pickle of your choice

This is the simplest thing—at most, all you need is to take some time to cook the onions. Put the oil and butter into a pan and when the butter has melted, add your onions. Cook for 5 minutes on medium to high heat until the onions are soft, then add the sugar and cook for another 5 minutes. You can also use crisp fried onions. Just omit the oil and use the butter only, on low heat, as the fried onions already have oil in them and just need warming through.

Once the onions are a deep brown, you are good to go. Mix in the cod roe, chile powder, curry powder, and garam masala, then, pressing down with the back of a wooden spoon, cook for another 5 minutes, until the mixture looks bone dry and the spices are well combined.

Put the cod roe mixture into a food processor along with the cream and blitz until you have a smooth paste. You may need to add another couple of tablespoons of cream to get it really smooth.

The trickiest bit is deciding how much you will eat, how much you will save, and what will be frozen. I like to eat my pâté warm with crispbreads and some sweet eggplant pickle. But before tucking in, take the time to transfer some into freezer-safe tubs so you have pâté whenever you want—or it can be cooled, kept in the fridge, and used as a sandwich spread (bring back to room temperature before serving).

The pâté will keep in the fridge for 3 days. Freeze leftovers in a tub or freezer bag.

SERVES: 4+   TOTAL TIME: 30–40 MINUTES

Anything eaten between two bits of bread is a winner. I always buy these enormous mushrooms and feel sad when I chop them up. They are so big and bold and it seems natural to keep them as they are. So here these massive mushrooms are broiled whole with loads of butter and loaded with mozzarella. Add some brioche and horseradish cream and you don't even need any sides.

MUSHROOM MOZZARELLA BURGERS

6 portobello mushrooms, any long stalks trimmed

½ cup plus 1 tablespoon garlic butter (you can buy this, but to make your own just mix some softened butter with 1 teaspoon of granulated garlic)

6 brioche burger buns, halved

2 large mozzarella balls, sliced into 6 large disks

6 tablespoons horseradish cream

arugula, to serve

You will need a baking sheet large enough to fit the 12 burger bun halves.

Preheat the broiler on the highest setting or preheat the oven to 400°F/ 200°C. Place the mushrooms on the sheet, with the underside facing upward. This will allow for the butter to be soaked into the little gaps between the gills. Mushrooms are like sponges, and if they are going to soak anything up it should be garlic butter.

Divide the garlic butter between the 6 mushrooms and broil for 5 minutes, until the butter has melted and the mushrooms are slightly shriveled.

Remove from the oven and pop a bun bottom on top of each mushroom to soak up all that butter. Once the butter has soaked into the bread, remove the bun bottom and divide the mozzarella slices among the mushrooms. Put the bun bottom back on and flip over, so that you now have the dome of the mushroom facing upward.

Put the burger bun tops on the same sheet, cut side facing up, and broil for 2 minutes. Watch over them, as the brioche bread can toast very quickly. If you can't fit them all on, toast the tops on a separate sheet for 1 to 2 minutes.

Remove from the oven, spread each bun top with some horseradish cream, and add a small handful of arugula leaves. Pop the top on the bottom and the burgers are ready to eat.

This is a messy eat and loaded with butter, but I wouldn't have it any other way, so enjoy it with a napkin. If you are saving these or have some left over, which I always do, they make great lunches. Wrap them individually in foil and reheat when you need them.

If you are saving some for the week ahead, be sure not to include the arugula leaves, as they will wilt and not taste very good.

If you are making your own garlic butter, double the quantity and keep it in the fridge—it's handy for lots of other dishes.

SERVES: 6   ACTIVE TIME: 10 MINUTES   TOTAL TIME: 15 MINUTES

I never ate sausages until I was about twenty-four. I was always curious, but I could never find any halal sausages, and then, when I did find them, they were always in huge packs of sixteen. So I always cooked more than I needed, even after having a full English breakfast. This is a simple cut-corners-type sausage and mash with all the fragrance of Bengali five-spice. I would put the spice in everything if I could, but I won't. However, it does very well in this recipe, when you occasionally bite into a whole spice. We make two here—one for now and one for your freezer.

BENGALI BANGERS AND HASH SMASH

2 x 1½-lb packs of frozen hash browns

2 tablespoons vegetable oil

½ teaspoon Bengali Spice Mix (Panch Phoran— see p. 237)

16 sausages, cut in half lengthwise (I like chicken sausages, but you can use your faves)

⅔ cup onion chutney/ marmalade

½ teaspoon chile powder

1 teaspoon salt

2½ cups hot water

3 tablespoons gravy granules

6 tablespoons mayonnaise

1 teaspoon chile flakes

1 tablespoon dried cilantro, or a small handful of fresh cilantro, finely chopped

3½ oz extra-sharp Cheddar cheese, grated

Start by putting the hash browns into a microwave-safe bowl and defrosting them in the microwave for 10 minutes. You may need to do this in two batches.

Heat the oil in a large nonstick pan. When it's hot, add the Bengali spice mix and, as soon as the whole spices start to pop, add the sausages and allow them to cook for about 5 minutes, until they are golden and slightly curled.

Now add the onion chutney, chile powder, and salt and mix thoroughly. Stir in the hot water and, as soon as it comes to a boil, add the gravy granules and stir them in. The mixture should start to thicken straight away. Let simmer gently for 10 minutes.

Meanwhile, put the hash browns into another large nonstick frying pan or a large, deep wok over medium heat and use a spoon to break them up into small chunks. As the edges start to crisp up a little, stir in the mayonnaise—this will make it creamy and help the spices to stick. Add the chile flakes and cilantro and mix well.

Dinner is ready, but first, put half the sausage mixture into an oven-safe dish (approx. 10 x 8 inches/25 x 20cm) so you can freeze it for another time. Add just a few spoons of the gravy and top with half the hash brown mixture. Set aside to cool completely before freezing.

Now you can have dinner. Serve sprinkled with the cheese.

To reheat, preheat the oven to 350°F/180°C and bake for 40 minutes from frozen, keeping it covered all the time, except for the last 5 minutes.

The reason why I love this recipe so much is that I always know I will get two for one here. The roast chicken is in a pan and the couscous is cooked in the same one. What I never do is throw the carcass away, because that is full of lovely shreds of meat and juices from the bones and with that I make my chicken soup.

ROAST CHICKEN WITH LEMON COUSCOUS

1 x 3¾ lb whole chicken

a drizzle of oil

salt and pepper

5 small red onions, peeled and quartered

3 preserved lemons, halved

10 anchovy fillets

1½ cups pearl couscous

2 cups boiling water

a large handful of fresh parsley, chopped

Heat the oven to 400°F/200°C.

Put the chicken into a roasting dish, drizzle generously with oil, and sprinkle liberally with salt and pepper. Add the onions, preserved lemons, and anchovy fillets, then cover with foil and cook for 1 hour 15 minutes.

Take the dish out of the oven and take off the foil, then move the chicken to one side of the dish and bring the ingredients on the bottom of the pan together. Squash the lemons and anchovies with the back of a fork. Stir in the couscous, then pour in the boiling water and give it a stir. Pop the dish back into the oven for another 15 minutes, uncovered.

Take out of the oven again and let rest for 10 minutes to allow the moisture to absorb into the couscous and the chicken to rest. Stir in the parsley.

Carve the chicken and serve with the couscous.

CHICKEN SOUP

Once dinner is done, collect the carcass and all the bones and pop them into a large pan, along with 1½ quarts of cold water. Peel and quarter 2 medium potatoes (about 1 lb 2 oz) and drop those straight in, along with 1 teaspoon of garlic paste, ½ teaspoon of salt, and 2 tablespoons of dried tarragon. Bring to a boil, then lower the heat and cook gently on medium heat for at least 1 hour with the lid on the pan. The chicken on the carcass should be soft and the potatoes so soft they should be falling apart.

Take the bones out, then take off all the chicken meat and put it back into the pan. Use the back of a fork to squash the potatoes down a little—this will thicken the soup. This is a good base if you want to add the odd vegetable or two and simmer until tender; otherwise it is ready to eat.

If you have any leftovers, this soup freezes really well.

SERVES: 4–6   ACTIVE TIME: 5 MINUTES   TOTAL TIME: 1 HOUR 45 MINUTES

This is something I used to cook for my kids when they were much younger, and I still make it sometimes among the floods of recipes that I test. I don't like spaghetti hoops as they are, neat out of the can, but I can really appreciate their sweetness and ability to bulk out a dish when they are mixed with other things. So this is exactly that—lots of white fish, mixed with a few vegetable-drawer staples and canned hoops and topped with breadcrumbs. If you're making one of these, it's worth making two, as we do here, so that one can sit in your freezer until next time.

HOOP FISH BAKE

2 x 13-oz pollock fillets, defrosted and chopped into bite-size chunks

10 cherry tomatoes, halved, or 2 tomatoes, chopped

3 green onions, finely chopped

2 red chiles, thinly sliced

7 florets of broccoli, chopped roughly (or you could use defrosted frozen broccoli, with all the moisture squeezed out)

1 teaspoon salt

1 teaspoon smoked paprika

2 x 13.5-oz/385g cans of spaghetti hoops, such as SpaghettiOs, drained

FOR THE BREADCRUMB TOPPING

4 small slices of bread or 2 large (approx. 3½ oz)

1 teaspoon granulated garlic

½ teaspoon salt

3 tablespoons olive oil

Have two oven- and freezer-safe dishes, approx. 8 x 10-inch/20 x 25cm, at the ready. I like to use the ones that have plastic lids.

Preheat the oven to 350°F/180°C.

Start by putting the fish into a bowl—if there is too much liquid, squeeze out any extra water by hand so the dish doesn't end up being too wet.

Add the chopped tomatoes, green onions, chiles, and broccoli and mix together. Stir in the salt and paprika, then mix in the drained hoops.

Divide the mixture equally between the two dishes and level the top.

To make the breadcrumb topping, put the bread, garlic granules, salt, and oil into a food processor and whiz until you have fine crumbs. Top each dish with half the breadcrumbs and bake for 30 minutes.

Serve one dish as soon as it comes out of the oven, and allow the other one to cool completely, then cover and freeze.

SERVES: 4   ACTIVE TIME: 30 MINUTES   TOTAL TIME: 1 HOUR

Growing up in Luton, you can't often make chicken and fries as good as the ones that come out of the chicken shop that's open until 3 a.m. But when time is short and with kids looking up at me, I like to try, and God loves a trier. Nothing about this feels like takeout, but I love chicken and potatoes any which way. This is how I cook them in the week, but they're great for summer weekend barbecues too.

PIRI DRUMSTICKS, FRIES, AND PEA MASH

FOR THE CHICKEN

10 chicken drumsticks, with the skin still on

1 x 1½-oz jar of paprika

1 x 1½-oz jar of chile powder

1 x ½-oz jar of dried oregano

1 x ½-oz jar of ground ginger

1 x 1½-oz jar of granulated garlic

1 x 1½-oz jar of granulated onion

5 tablespoons salt

4 teaspoons vegetable oil, for roasting

1 lb 2 oz frozen oven fries

FOR THE PEA MASH

2½ cups frozen peas

1 teaspoon ginger paste

1 small red onion, finely chopped

a sprinkling of salt

1 lemon, juice and finely grated zest

a handful of fresh cilantro

Score the drumsticks, cutting through the skin and just a little bit into the flesh. Pop them into a pan and pour in enough boiling water to cover them completely. Put the pan on the stovetop and bring to a boil, then lower the heat and let simmer for 10 minutes.

Meanwhile, make the piri sprinkle by putting the paprika, chile powder, oregano, ginger, garlic granules, onion granules, and salt into a screwtop jar. Put the lid on and give it a good shake to mix everything together.

Preheat the oven to 425°F/220°C.

Put the oven fries on a baking sheet. Drain the drumsticks and put them into a roasting dish. Pat the chicken dry with paper towels, then drizzle with the oil and massage it into the chicken when it's cool enough to handle.

Sprinkle the spice mix over the drumsticks, using enough to make a generous coating. Put them into the oven, along with the sheet of frozen fries, and bake for 20 to 25 minutes. Or, if you're doing the drumsticks on the barbecue, put them on for 10 to 15 minutes, until cooked through.

Meanwhile, make the pea mash. Defrost the peas by pouring boiling water over them. This should only take a minute. Drain the peas and put them into a bowl, then, using the back of a fork or a rolling pin, lightly crush them with the ginger paste, chopped onion, salt, lemon juice and zest, and cilantro.

By the time the mash is made, the chicken and fries will be ready to serve. Set aside 4 drumsticks to cool, so they can be frozen in a tub or bag and eaten on another occasion.

SERVES: 4   TOTAL TIME: 45 MINUTES

We were in Canada not long ago and one of the first things I asked when I went there was, "What shall we eat?" The same question we always ask ourselves. So many of our breaks are dictated by what we will eat. Canada didn't disappoint. Poutine is a Canadian *thing*, and quite a thing it is too. I love fries and it turns out so do they, but with curd cheese and mushroom gravy. So that's what I'm doing here. Anywhere where they adorn their fries in this way is a place I intend to revisit, but, until then, it happens in my kitchen.

POUTINE

2 tablespoons vegetable oil

2 tablespoons garlic paste

2 cups frozen onions, or 2 medium onions, chopped

1 tablespoon salt

1 lb 10 oz button mushrooms, quartered

1 teaspoon dried rosemary

1 teaspoon dried thyme

1 quart vegetable stock (1 quart boiling water mixed with 4 stock cubes)

1 tablespoon nutritional yeast

¼ cup cornstarch

1 tablespoon cocoa powder

1½ lb oven fries

1 lb 2 oz halloumi cheese, diced into small ½-inch pieces

Begin by making the gravy. I'm making more than I need, as this gravy is great for freezing, so you don't have to make it again when you need it, be it for your poutine or your Sunday roast.

Heat the oil in a large pan, then add the garlic and onions, along with the salt, and cook on high heat until the onions are soft but a deep golden brown. If it starts to stick, add a splash of water.

Stir in the mushrooms, rosemary, and thyme, then add the stock and nutritional yeast and bring to a boil.

Mix the cornstarch and cocoa with 3 tablespoons of water in a bowl, then add to the mushrooms and simmer gently while you cook the fries per the package instructions.

Have the halloumi cubes ready to serve. Once the gravy is thick, take it off the heat and use an immersion blender to make it smooth. That's the way I remember it, but if you want a chunky version, that's okay too.

Serve a heap of fries, sprinkle with the halloumi, and drench in the mushroom gravy.

Whatever gravy you have left, cool and freeze.

SERVES: 4   TOTAL TIME: 50 MINUTES

What I want to do one day is write a book about the versatility of the fish stick. There's something about these perfectly rectangular, golden fishy beauties that I cannot resist. So I have found yet another way to eat them. For all the times you may have thought, "I only have a box of fish sticks in the freezer," think of all the things you could have done. Enchiladas for one. We are making two batches with this recipe. One for dinner now, one for later on in the week or month. Just halve the ingredients if you prefer to only make today's.

FISH STICK ENCHILADAS

20 fish sticks, defrosted

2 small red onions, thinly sliced

1 x 11½-oz can of sweet corn kernels

3½ oz full-fat cream cheese

1 teaspoon freshly ground black pepper

8 flour tortillas

2 cups uncooked tomato purée

1 teaspoon salt

1 teaspoon chile flakes

1 teaspoon granulated garlic

1 teaspoon dried basil

7 oz Cheddar cheese, grated

Preheat the oven to 400°F/200°C, and have two baking dishes at the ready.

Put the defrosted fish sticks into a bowl and crush gently, using the back of a fork. Add the sliced onions, then mix in the corn, cream cheese, and black pepper.

Spread the tortillas out and divide the fish mixture between them. Fold and roll so you can get 4 of them into the dish comfortably, then arrange those in the dish, seam-side down.

To make the sauce, put the tomato purée into a bowl with the salt, chile flakes, garlic granules, and basil and mix well.

Spoon half the sauce all over the wraps in the dish and sprinkle with half the cheese.

Bake in the oven for 35 to 40 minutes, until the fish sticks are cooked and the cheese is bubbly. Serve with salad.

Put the other 4 filled tortillas into a freezer-safe baking dish, add the rest of the sauce and cheese, then cover the dish with foil and pop into the freezer.

I love fish, mostly when it is teamed up with citrus, and this is my take on that combination, using marmalade, which most of us have knocking about the house. It's fresh and zingy and although it sounds unusual, it tastes good. You can use fresh new potatoes instead, if you prefer—they should take the same amount of time to cook as the canned variety.

MARMALADE HADDOCK

2 x 19½-oz cans of new potatoes, drained and halved

3 sun-dried tomatoes (the antipasti kind, in oil), snipped into strips, plus 1 tablespoon oil from the jar

a drizzle of balsamic vinegar, about 1 tablespoon

a pinch of salt

4 haddock fillets

FOR THE TOPPING

6 tablespoons marmalade

1 teaspoon salt

2 teaspoons garlic paste

2 teaspoons chile flakes

¼ cup dried dill

1 cup panko breadcrumbs

Preheat the oven to 425°F/220°C.

Put the halved potatoes into a large roasting dish, along with the tomatoes, oil, balsamic, and salt, and give it all a really good stir. Place in the oven for 10 to 15 minutes to warm the potatoes through.

To make the topping, put the marmalade, salt, garlic paste, chile flakes, dill, and breadcrumbs into a food processor and whiz everything together. Take half the mixture and spread it all over the fish. Put the rest of the topping into a freezer bag and freeze, ready for the next time you need breadcrumbs for fish or chicken.

Take the dish of potatoes out of the oven and place the fish on top. Put back into the oven and bake for 15 minutes, until the fish is cooked and the topping is crunchy.

Freeze any leftovers in a tub.

Nut butters are so versatile, especially peanut, and whenever I run out, I just make my own. It's cheaper and so much easier. And it can be used for much more than just sandwiches—it's great with chicken and even better when you can have it for dinner. You make enough here to have a jar in your cupboard too.

ONE-PAN PEANUT CHICKEN

FOR THE PEANUT BUTTER

3½ cups salted peanuts

1 teaspoon salt (optional—you may find it salty enough with the salted peanuts)

1 tablespoon honey

4–5 tablespoons vegetable oil

FOR THE CHICKEN

9 oz gnocchi

2 lb 2 oz skinless, boneless chicken thighs, thinly sliced

¼ cup honey

¼ cup vegetable oil

5 tablespoons Thai Green Curry Paste (see p. 238)

5 tablespoons peanut butter

1 teaspoon salt

2 heads of broccoli, cut into florets

2 small red onions, cut into small wedges

3 tablespoons salted peanuts, roughly chopped

a handful of fresh cilantro, roughly chopped

juice of 1 lime

To make the peanut butter, put the nuts into a food processor with the salt and honey and blitz till the whole thing starts to change texture. Add the oil slowly and watch as it turns to butter before your very eyes. As soon as it's smooth and shiny, stop and transfer the mixture to a jar.

Preheat the oven to 400°F/200°C and have a roasting dish (about 13 x 9 x 2 inches/30 x 23 x 5cm) at the ready.

Bring a pot of water to a boil, then add the gnocchi. Boil until they come to the surface, then take off the heat, drain, and set aside.

Put the chicken into a large bowl. Add the honey, oil, curry paste, peanut butter, and salt, and mix it all well with your hands, massaging in all that flavor. Then put it into the roasting dish along with the broccoli, onions, and gnocchi and bake for 30 minutes, giving it a stir halfway through.

Serve topped with the chopped nuts, cilantro, and a squeeze of lime.

Freeze any leftovers in a tub or freezer bag.

SERVES: 4   ACTIVE TIME: 20 MINUTES   TOTAL TIME: 50 MINUTES

When I was younger, I had only ever seen the word *dansak* written on Dad's restaurant menus, and I used to watch the dish sizzling past me on a hot plate. We didn't eat curries like that at home. But now I always enjoy the wholesome, thick nature of a dansak—it's hearty, warm, and full of flavor. It's great if someone else is making it, but when I'm doing it, I want to make it quickly and often in double portions, so that I can enjoy it twice for half the work.

LAMB DANSAK

7 tablespoons butter

5 tablespoons vegetable oil

2 tablespoons garlic paste

2 tablespoons ginger paste

7 oz chopped onions

1 tablespoon salt

2 tablespoons chile paste

1 tablespoon tomato paste

1 tablespoon curry powder

2 tablespoons garam masala

1 teaspoon ground cinnamon

2 lb 2 oz lamb (neck, shoulder, or leg), diced into small cubes

2 x 15-oz cans of kidney beans, drained

TO SERVE

rice

heavy cream

fresh cilantro, chopped

Put the butter into a large pan with the oil and let it melt. Then turn up the heat, add the garlic paste, ginger paste, onions, and salt, and cook on high heat until the onions are very brown and soft. Keep a glass of water handy in case they start to stick—if they do, just splash in a little water.

Add the chile paste, tomato paste, curry powder, garam masala, and ground cinnamon, and cook on medium heat until the mixture really starts to thicken.

Add the lamb and let cook till the lamb is browned. Then put a lid on the pan and let it cook gently for 10 minutes.

In the meantime, put the drained kidney beans into a bowl and give them a little squash with the end of a rolling pin to help them break up a little. Dansak is traditionally made with lentils, but lentils take longer, so I use canned kidney beans instead—plus I love that deep purple color. Stir the beans into the lamb, pop the lid on again, and cook for 20 minutes over medium heat.

Cook some rice now, or, if you are still short on time, get a few of those precooked rice packages into the microwave.

I like to serve this with a tiny splash of cream drizzled on top and some chopped cilantro. A pineapple salsa also works as a refreshing side—just toss chunks of pineapple with chopped red chiles, red onion, and fresh cilantro.

Remember, there is enough curry here for two meals, so you can freeze the leftovers.

SERVES: 4   TOTAL TIME: 50 MINUTES

There's nothing I like more than eating a pasty the size of my head. I've only visited Cornwall a handful of times, but during those times the variations in pasties were shocking. I had a good go at trying as many as possible, learning the basics, the traditions, and the out-there flavors. They were filled with everything from chocolate to tikka! Some had butter pastry, others were more bready; some pleased, others depressed. So here I have taken the traditional flavors and kind of changed it around a bit, and changed the way I do it too. Make some now, save some for another day, but I applaud you if you can consume three human-head-sized pasties in one sitting!

SHORTCUT BEEF PASTIES

2 small red onions, diced

1 medium potato, grated

2 small parsnips, grated

2 sheets of defrosted puff pastry

1 egg, beaten

salt and pepper

8 oz ground beef

4 knobs of butter (about 1 tablespoon each)

Put the onions into a large bowl. I like using red onions, because they add a tiny bit of color, not so much once they are cooked but enough to see a slight difference, along with the lovely onion flavor. That onion flavor is one of my favorite parts of the whole pasty.

Traditionally the contents of a pasty would be thinly sliced, but to ensure that everything is cooked all the way through, I am grating the potato and parsnip instead. Take the grated potato and squeeze out any excess liquid, then add to the bowl of onions. Add the grated parsnips—I know these are not traditional, but they still add a lovely sweetness, plus I prefer grating parsnips (rutabagas are a bit fiddly).

Preheat the oven to 400°F/200°C and have a large baking sheet standing by.

Unroll the pastry and cut both sheets in half crosswise. Brush the edges of the pastry lightly with a little of the beaten egg.

Give the onion mixture a stir, then divide between the 4 pieces of pastry, piled high on one half, leaving the other half free, as you need to fold it over. Season generously with salt and pepper. Divide the ground beef into four portions and pile on top of the vegetables. Season well again. Add a knob of butter to each pile of filling.

Carefully fold over the pastry and press to seal the edges, then brush each pasty with more of the beaten egg and sprinkle the top with salt. Cut a slit in the top to allow steam out. Now bake in the oven for 35 to 40 minutes. Give it a breath before you eat it, as it will be really hot.

SERVES: 4, OR UP TO 8 IF YOU HAVE LITTLE MOUTHS TO FEED   ACTIVE TIME: 30 MINUTES   TOTAL TIME: 1 HOUR 15 MINUTES

My mission in life is to eat every kind of fry, and it would be rude not to share my ideas or experiences with you. I recently watched a show where they served lava fries in an American diner, and I was like, "That's it, I'm making those." They are spicy, hot, and mountain-like, dripping with chili and sour cream. The slow descent of the sauce down the fries makes them look like an erupting volcano. This is not for the fainthearted. There's enough here to freeze some for another day.

LAVA FRIES

1 lb 10 oz frozen oven fries

FOR THE MASALA BEEF

5 tablespoons vegetable oil

10 cloves of garlic, crushed

2 medium onions, finely diced

1 tablespoon salt

2 lb 2 oz ground beef

3 tablespoons chile paste

2 tablespoons tomato paste

1 tablespoon paprika

1 tablespoon chile flakes

1 tablespoon ground cumin

1 tablespoon ground coriander

½ x 10-oz bottle of Worcestershire sauce

2 x 11-oz cans of tomato soup

fresh cilantro, chopped

1 x 15-oz can of kidney beans, drained (for the chili)

FOR THE TOPPING

1¼ cups sour cream

3 tablespoons whole milk

2 tablespoons granulated onion

1 tablespoon granulated garlic

1 teaspoon salt

1 x 7½-oz jar of jalapeños, drained and finely chopped

3½ oz Cheddar cheese, grated

Preheat the oven ready to cook the fries, according to the instructions on the package. Then start making the masala beef. Put the oil into a large pan on high heat. Add the garlic, and as soon as it starts to brown, add the onions and salt and cook until the onions are golden and soft.

Add the ground beef and cook until browned, then add the chile paste, tomato paste, paprika, chile flakes, cumin, coriander, and Worcestershire sauce, and cook for 5 minutes.

Pour in the tomato soup, stir, then let simmer on medium heat until the mixture is very thick, stirring occasionally.

Now pop the fries into the preheated oven and cook as instructed.

Make the topping by mixing the sour cream with the milk, onion granules, garlic granules, and salt.

To finish the masala beef, stir in the cilantro. Divide the mixture in half and mix in the kidney beans to make a chili for another day.

Once the fries are done, pile them up in an oven-safe serving dish. Pile the masala beef on top of them, sprinkle with the jalapeños, then scatter the cheese and broil on high until the top is toasted. Remove from the oven and serve with the topping.

Allow leftover masala beef to cool, then freeze in a tub or bag. You could serve it another day with rice and sour cream, sprinkled with fresh cilantro and chopped chiles.

SERVES: 4   TOTAL TIME: 1 HOUR

I like the idea of having an alternative to chicken, and for us, a leg of lamb is a real treat. A butterflied leg of lamb is basically a leg of lamb with the bone taken out, which makes it easier to cook and easier to carve, as there's no bone to cut around. Perfect for the oven and even better on the barbecue. Cooked simply, it's finished with a fragrant rhubarb and rosemary glaze.

BUTTERFLIED LAMB LEG WITH A RHUBARB AND ROSEMARY GLAZE

whole leg of lamb, butterflied (you can get your butcher to do this, or buy it already done)

olive oil, for coating

2 tablespoons salt

FOR THE RHUBARB GLAZE

4 tablespoons butter

2 large sprigs of rosemary, leaves removed from stems and finely chopped

4 cloves of garlic, chopped

14 oz rhubarb, thinly sliced

½ teaspoon salt

2 tablespoons honey

1 teaspoon chile powder

Start by preheating the oven to 350°F/180°C. If the leg of lamb is thicker in places, lay it on a board and make vertical slits, then open it up. This will help it to cook evenly.

Pop the lamb into a large roasting dish. Drizzle it with oil and be generous. Cover both sides. Sprinkle with the salt and, again, don't be afraid to be generous—that's a big bit of meat and it needs seasoning well.

Pop it into the oven for 40 minutes if you like the meat medium, or 30 minutes if you prefer it pink. While it's cooking, make the glaze.

Melt the butter in a pan. Next, add the rosemary and garlic and cook on high heat for just a few minutes. Lower the heat to medium and add the rhubarb, salt, honey, and chile powder, then stir.

Increase the heat slightly and mix occasionally. As it cooks it should resemble lava bubbling. You need to cook this for about 30 to 40 minutes, until you have a rich, deep paste. If it starts to stick, just lower the heat and stir frequently. If you have a particularly tart batch of rhubarb, you might like to add an extra 1 to 2 tablespoons of honey.

Once the leg of lamb has been in the oven for the required cooking time, remove it. If there is any liquid in the bottom of the roasting dish, carefully drain it off.

SERVES: 4-8 BASED ON A 2 LB 2 OZ LEG OF LAMB

ACTIVE TIME: 30 MINUTES   TOTAL TIME: 1 HOUR 45 MINUTES

Brush the glaze all over the top and sides of the meat, return to the oven, and leave it fat-side up to finish cooking.

Once the lamb has cooked for another 20 minutes, take it out and let it rest for at least 15 minutes before eating.

TO BARBECUE

Alternatively, you can barbecue the butterflied lamb—it's always good to have options. Once the coals are hot enough, put the seasoned and oiled lamb on the barbecue, fat-side down, and cook on high heat for 5 minutes, until well browned. Turn over and cook for 5 minutes to brown the other side too.

Now move the coals from the center to around the edges of the barbecue and let the meat cook, covered, for 30 to 40 minutes, turning occasionally if you need to.

Take the lamb off the barbecue, cover it with foil, and let it rest for 15 minutes, undisturbed. By which time it is ready to slice and eat.

Sometimes we like to go meat-free during the week, and that's when mushrooms are my saving grace. They are deep in color and rich in flavor—they give off the aura of meat, but they are not. That's why we love them, and it means we can have a meat-free lasagne too. This is the kind of thing you want to put in the slow cooker just before popping out, knowing you will have dinner ready for when you get back and another one ready to go in the freezer (if you only want to make one, halve all of the ingredients).

SLOW COOKER MUSHROOM LASAGNE

½ cup vegetable oil

8 cloves of garlic, crushed

2 medium onions, diced

2 teaspoons salt

2 heaped teaspoons cumin seeds

2 x 1 lb 6 oz packages of button mushrooms, roughly sliced, or 4 x 10-oz cans of mushrooms

4 teaspoons freshly ground black pepper

2¼ cups mascarpone

¾ cup plus 2 tablespoons whole milk

14 oz Cheddar cheese, grated

cooking oil spray

12 lasagne sheets

Put the oil into a medium pan on high heat and as soon as it is hot, add the garlic. When it's golden, add the onions and salt and cook until soft.

Add the cumin seeds, then add the mushrooms and keep cooking on high until they have really reduced in size. Stir in the black pepper and cook until most of the moisture has evaporated, then take off the heat.

To make the easy white sauce, mix together the mascarpone, milk, and cheese.

Lightly spray some oil on the inside of your slow cooker pot, and have a medium lasagne dish at the ready.

Put a quarter of the mushroom mixture into the slow cooker and the other quarter into the lasagne dish, then make a layer of 3 sheets of lasagne in each, breaking the pasta up where necessary to fit.

Layer on a quarter of the mascarpone sauce in the slow cooker, and another quarter in the lasagne dish, followed by the rest of the mushroom mixture and the remaining lasagne sheets, half in each. Finally, spread the rest of the mascarpone mixture on top. Set the lasagne dish aside to cool. Cook the lasagne in the slow cooker on low for 2 hours.

I like to serve this with garlic bread (see p. 242) and salad.

When the lasagne in the dish has cooled, cover with foil and freeze.

SERVES: 4 NOW AND 4 LATER   ACTIVE TIME: 40 MINUTES   TOTAL TIME: 2 HOURS 30 MINUTES

From my travels through Thailand this is a recipe that has stayed with me—it's fragrant, creamy and spicy, warming and delicious. I don't know whose grandmother started this, but whoever she is, we are thankful, because it is one of the best things ever to pass my lips. The paste is pretty versatile—see opposite for other ways you can use it.

GRANDMAMA'S CURRY

FOR THE CURRY PASTE

1⅔ cups dried shredded coconut

⅓ cup whole peppercorns

3 whole heads of garlic, peeled

9 oz ginger, peeled and chopped

4½ oz fresh red chiles, roughly chopped

9 sticks of lemongrass

5 teaspoons ground turmeric

¼ cup salt

1¼ cups vegetable oil (you may need more)

TO COOK

1 cup dried shredded coconut

¼ cup curry paste (see above) per 2 cups water

2 tablespoons garlic paste

2 tablespoons ginger paste

1 cup coconut cream

1 whole chicken, skin removed

about 1½ quarts water

2 tablespoons cornstarch

7 oz snow peas

7 oz baby corn, halved lengthwise

TO SERVE

rice

a large handful of fresh cilantro, chopped

limes, cut into quarters

Start by making the curry paste. Toast the coconut in a dry pan over medium heat until very brown. Put into a blender with the peppercorns, and blend until the peppercorns are broken down. Add the garlic, ginger, chiles, lemongrass, turmeric, salt, and oil. Blend till you have a smooth paste. If it isn't moving, scrape the sides down and add some more oil until it does.

Transfer the curry paste to a large jar. This makes a large amount, and it will keep in the fridge for 6 months.

Put the 1 cup of dried shredded coconut into a large pot and toast until dark brown. Take off the heat and stir in the ¼ cup curry paste, then add the garlic paste, ginger paste, and the coconut cream and mix really well.

Add the whole chicken to the pot and pour in the water—you need enough to come about three-quarters of the way up the chicken. Bring to a boil, then lower the heat and let the whole thing cook gently for 1 hour.

Take off the heat and use a slotted spoon to remove the chicken, gently, as it will be falling apart. Place it on a large plate or a board. While the chicken is cooling slightly, turn up the heat under the liquid in the pot and boil rapidly for 10 to 15 minutes.

Pull the chicken off the bones, using two forks as it will be hot, and get rid of the bones. Put the chicken back into the pot and cook slowly for another 30 minutes with the lid off.

Meanwhile cook enough rice for 6 people.

Mix the cornstarch with 3 tablespoons of water in a small bowl, then stir it into the sauce for the last 5 minutes of cooking, together with the snow peas and baby corn.

Put the rice on a platter and pour all the chicken curry on top. Sprinkle with chopped cilantro and serve with wedges of lime.

Leftovers can be frozen in a tub or freezer bag.

GRANDMAMA'S CURRY PASTE

Once you have a curry paste made up, the possibilities are practically endless. This paste is really versatile. It is a great base for any curry—be adventurous with the protein you choose—use fish, lamb, or chunks of good, hearty vegetables. It's also great added to instant noodles for extra flavor, and can simply be drunk as a flavored broth by stirring 1 teaspoon of the paste into a mug of boiling water.

These do take a little effort to make, and they can get demolished in seconds, but most of the effort is in waiting around. Lots of waiting. But it's worth it—these buns are soft and light, and with the spicy raw tuna it is quite literally a melt-in-the-mouth experience.

BAO BUNS WITH SPICY TUNA

FOR THE BUNS

4 cups/500g all-purpose flour

2 teaspoons salt

2 tablespoons sugar

2 teaspoons fast-acting instant yeast

1¼ cups/300ml warm water

vegetable oil, for brushing

FOR THE SPICY TUNA

1 lb/440g tuna steaks (sashimi grade), finely chopped

2 green onions, finely chopped

1 red chile, finely diced, with seeds

1-inch/2.5cm piece of ginger, peeled and grated

2 tablespoons honey

5 tablespoons soy sauce

2 teaspoons sesame oil

1 tablespoon black or white sesame seeds

a small handful of fresh cilantro, chopped

Put the flour, salt, sugar, and yeast into a bowl and mix together. Make a well in the center and add the water, then bring the dough together. If you're using a mixer, knead for 5 minutes on high speed, and if you're doing it by hand, knead for 10 minutes. The dough should be lovely and shiny and stretchy. Place back in the bowl and let rise for 1 hour, covered, in a warm place until doubled in size.

Meanwhile cut out 10 squares of parchment paper measuring 4 x 4 inches/10 x 10cm and have two baking sheets at the ready.

Roll the dough into a sausage shape and cut it into 10 equal pieces (3 oz/80g each). Roll each one out to a circle ¼ inch/5mm in thickness and brush all over with oil. Brush a chopstick with oil too, then lay it in the center, fold over the dough to create a semicircle, and pull the stick out. Place on a piece of paper and then on a baking sheet. Do this to all 10 pieces of dough, then cover with a piece of greased plastic wrap and let rest for 30 minutes, until doubled in size.

Depending on the size of your steamer, steam as many buns as you can at a time without overcrowding them. They should take 5 to 6 minutes, until springy to touch.

While the buns are steaming, make the spicy tuna. Put the chopped tuna into a bowl and add the onions, chile, ginger, honey, soy sauce, sesame oil, sesame seeds, and chopped cilantro. Snap open the steamed buns and fill them with the spicy tuna.

HANDY TIP

Any leftover tuna mix can be saved in the fridge for the next day, to have with rice, a stir-fry, or in a poke bowl, and any leftover buns can be frozen.

ACTIVE TIME: 45 MINUTES   TOTAL TIME: 2 HOURS 15 MINUTES

Jackfruit is all the rage at the moment, which is bizarre, because I have been eating the stuff my whole entire life and never batted an eyelid. I like it ripe on my toast, sweet and fragrant. But when still green and not sweet, it makes a great alternative to meat—with its stringy body and firm texture I kind of get it, and it is delicious in a curry.

JACKFRUIT CURRY WITH NO-YEAST NAAN

FOR THE CURRY

10 cloves of garlic

1¼-inch/3cm piece of ginger, peeled and chopped

1 medium onion

1 tablespoon salt

7 tablespoons/100ml vegetable oil

1 teaspoon ground cinnamon

1 teaspoon chile paste

1 tablespoon tomato paste

1 teaspoon ground turmeric

1 tablespoon curry powder

2 x 20-oz/565g cans of jackfruit in brine

¾ cup plus 2 tablespoons/ 200ml water

fresh cilantro, chopped

½ a lime

FOR THE NAAN

4 cups/500g all-purpose flour

2 tablespoons nigella seeds or any black seeds (black sesame, brown mustard, or poppy)

5 tablespoons sugar

1 teaspoon salt

1 teaspoon baking powder

1 cup/240ml whole milk

vegetable oil, for brushing

In a food processor, blitz the garlic, ginger, onion, and salt to a smooth paste. Add water if you need to, but very little.

Put the oil into a large nonstick pan over medium heat. Add the cinnamon and fry for 20 seconds. Then add the paste from the processor and cook for 5 minutes—if it starts to stick, add splashes of water. Stir in the chile paste, tomato paste, turmeric, and curry powder.

While that cooks on medium heat, drain the jackfruit and cut it into small, bite-size pieces. Add them to the pan, then stir in the water and let simmer gently until totally dry.

Now start on the naan. Mix the flour in a bowl with the nigella seeds, sugar, salt, and baking powder. Make a well in the center and add the milk, then use a spatula to bring the dough together. Knead on a floured surface for 10 minutes, or, if you are using a dough hook on a mixer, knead for 5 minutes. Then let the dough rest in the bowl for 10 minutes.

Preheat the oven to 450°F/240°C, and put a large baking sheet in to get hot.

Divide the dough into 8 equal portions, then roll them all out as thin as you can get them. Take the hot baking sheet out of the oven and brush its surface with oil. Add as many bits of rolled dough as will fit. Bake for 5 minutes, until lightly browned, and lightly brush the tops with oil once you have taken them out of the oven. Repeat until all the dough is cooked.

To finish the jackfruit curry, stir in the cilantro, drizzle with a squeeze of fresh lime juice, and you are ready to eat. There is enough here for 4 meals, so if you have any curry left over, you can freeze it for another day.

You can also freeze any leftover naan breads, or keep them for the next day to make Harissa Bean Pizza (see p. 22).

SERVES: 4   TOTAL TIME: 1 HOUR 10 MINUTES

Paneer is a kind of cheese that is creamy but meaty enough to withstand being rustled about and cooked furiously. So rather than using ground meat, I use blitzed paneer to make these cheesy koftas, dipped in an easy sauce, and served with hot vermicelli rice.

PANEER KOFTAS WITH VERMICELLI RICE

FOR THE KOFTAS

1 x 8-oz package of paneer

1 teaspoon salt

1 teaspoon cumin seeds

1 teaspoon chile flakes

3 cloves of garlic

1 small onion, roughly chopped

1 large egg

1 x 14-oz can of chickpeas, drained

½ cup chickpea flour

2 cups vegetable oil, for frying

FOR THE VERMICELLI RICE

3½ oz vermicelli

1 cinnamon stick

5 bay leaves

½ cup plus 2 tablespoons butter

2 cups basmati rice, rinsed and drained

1 teaspoon salt

1 quart boiling water

Begin by making the koftas. Put the paneer chunks into a food processor and whiz until they look minced. Now add the salt, cumin seeds, chile flakes, garlic, onion, egg, and chickpeas and keep whizzing until you can see that the chickpeas have broken down. Now add the chickpea flour and whiz until you have a very thick paste.

Put the oil into a small pot, making sure it comes halfway up. Have a baking sheet ready, lined with paper towels. Heat the oil on high heat, then lower to medium.

Drop heaped spoonfuls of the kofta mixture into the oil and fry for 3 to 4 minutes, making sure to turn them occasionally. Do this till you have finished them all. You should have enough koftas for half to be eaten for dinner now and the other half to be frozen, so set half of them aside to cool.

For the rice, put the vermicelli, cinnamon, and bay leaves into a dry pan and turn the heat up to medium. Toast the noodles for a few minutes, until they are very golden brown. Add the butter and let it melt.

Now add the rinsed rice, along with the salt, and cook for 2 minutes. Pour in the boiling water. Be very careful at this point, as it will hiss and spit when you pour it in. Keep stirring until it returns to a boil, and as soon as it does, keep on stirring until all the water evaporates. Lower the heat, pop a lid on the pan, and let steam for 15 minutes.

In the meantime make the sauce by mixing together the yogurt, tahini, garlic, ginger, maple syrup, curry powder, salt, and lime juice and zest in a bowl.

FOR THE SAUCE

1 cup Greek yogurt

½ cup tahini

2 cloves of garlic, crushed

1-inch piece of ginger, peeled and grated

1 tablespoon maple syrup

1 tablespoon curry powder

1 teaspoon salt

1 lime, juice and finely grated zest

TO SERVE

limes, cut into wedges

When the rice is cooked, serve it with the koftas, with the yogurt sauce alongside and wedges of lime.

This goes brilliantly with a simple tomato salad and some fresh cilantro.

Both the koftas and the rice can be frozen. Perfect as a sandwich filler or a nibble with a dip if you're having guests over or need a snack in front of the telly that isn't a bag of chips for a change.

If you have any sauce left, you can loosen it with some olive oil and use it as a salad dressing.

I was raised on fish curry, so brothy, flavorful fish is right up my alley. This is warm and delicious and perfect to dippy-dip with homemade garlic bread.

CHORIZO FISH STEW WITH GARLIC BREAD

FOR THE GARLIC BREAD

3⅔ cups/450g all-purpose flour

1 package (2¼ teaspoons/7g) fast-acting instant yeast

1 teaspoon sugar

1 teaspoon salt

¼ cup/50g salted butter

1¼ cups/300ml warm water

2 tablespoons coarse semolina

5 tablespoons/75g salted butter, melted

5 cloves of garlic, grated

fresh parsley, chopped

kosher salt or flaky salt

FOR THE STEW

5 tablespoons/75ml vegetable oil

8 oz/230g chorizo, chopped

2 tablespoons crushed mustard seeds

5 cloves of garlic, crushed

6 tomatoes, chopped

1 teaspoon salt

1 teaspoon tomato paste

1 teaspoon chile powder

5 tablespoons/75ml malt vinegar

1 lb 3 oz/540g white fish chunks (I like to use pollock or basa)

1¾ cups/450ml water

4½ oz/120g smoked salmon trimmings

fresh parsley, chopped

Start by making the garlic bread. Put the flour, yeast, sugar, and salt into a bowl. Add the butter and rub it in. Make a well in the center and add the water, then bring the dough together and knead for 10 minutes, until it is smooth and stretchy. Put it back into the bowl, cover, and let rise for 1 hour, or until the dough has doubled in size.

Have ready a roasting dish, lightly greased and with semolina sprinkled over the bottom. Knock the dough back in the bowl, then tip out on to a floured surface. Divide it into golfball-size pieces and put them in the dish, leaving small gaps in between to give the dough room to grow. Cover and let rise until doubled in size.

Now on to the stew. Put the oil into a pan over medium heat, and when it's hot add the chorizo and cook until some of the spices have been released. Add the mustard seeds and allow them to sizzle. Then add the garlic and cook until golden. Add the chopped tomatoes, salt, tomato paste, chile powder, and vinegar, and cook on medium heat for 10 minutes.

Preheat the oven to 325°F/160°C and bake the garlic bread for 40 to 45 minutes.

Now add your white fish to the stew and cook for a few minutes with the lid on. Then take off the lid, add the water, and let simmer on the lowest heat.

Take the stew off the heat and mix in the salmon and a large handful of parsley. Put the lid on the pan to keep it hot.

Meanwhile, add the melted butter, the garlic, a small handful of parsley, and a good pinch of salt. As soon as the rolls come out of the oven, brush all the butter on top of the hot rolls.

Serve the stew with the hot garlicky bread.

Note: You can double-batch the stew ingredients, if you like, so you can keep one batch in the freezer for another time.

SERVES: 4

ACTIVE TIME: 1 HOUR
TOTAL TIME: 2 HOURS 30 MINUTES

I ate these momos with cabbage on a mountain in Nepal a while ago. I have the flavor and memory of this beautiful dish etched in my mind and have desperately tried to recreate its magic. I hope I have done it justice. We make a double batch of the soy cabbage here, so you have a meal for another day. It tastes good with rice, as a filling for samosas or grilled cheese sandwiches, or cold from the fridge on a pasta salad.

TING MOMOS WITH SOY CABBAGE

FOR THE MOMO DOUGH

2 cups/250g all-purpose flour, plus a little extra for dusting

1 teaspoon salt

1 tablespoon sugar

1 teaspoon fast-acting instant yeast

½ cup plus 2 tablespoons/ 150ml warm water

vegetable oil, for greasing

FOR THE SOY CABBAGE

½ cup plus 2 tablespoons/ 150ml vegetable oil

2 teaspoons mustard seeds

2 teaspoons cumin seeds

2 teaspoons coriander seeds

1 tablespoon chile flakes

2 medium onions, diced

1 large head of garlic, peeled and crushed

2 teaspoons salt

2 red bell peppers, diced

1 white cabbage, finely shredded

1 lb 5 oz/600g texturized vegetable protein (or any vegetarian ground meat substitute of your choice)

1 teaspoon ground turmeric

Start by making the momo dough. Mix together the flour, salt, sugar, and yeast in a bowl. Make a well in the center and add the water, then bring the dough together. Knead for 10 minutes, until smooth, then rub the outside of the dough with a little oil. Grease the inside of a bowl with oil and put in the dough, then cover with plastic wrap or a tea towel and let rise for 1 hour, or until it has doubled in size.

Meanwhile, cook the cabbage. Put the oil into a large pan on medium to high heat. Add the mustard seeds, cumin seeds, and coriander seeds, and as soon as they start to pop, add the chile flakes and give it a quick stir.

Add the onions and turn the heat up to high. Let the onions cook, tossing them around in the oil and spices, until they are golden brown, stirring now and again. Turn the heat down to medium, then add the garlic and salt and cook for a few more minutes.

Add the red bell peppers and the shredded cabbage and give it all a stir, then add a small splash of water and put the lid on the pan. Decrease the heat to low and let steam for 30 minutes, allowing the cabbage to wilt.

Take the dough out of the bowl and put it on a very lightly floured surface. Oil your hands lightly, and oil a steamer basket generously all over. Flatten the dough and roll it out into a rectangle roughly 16 x 18 inches/ 40 x 45cm.

Oil the top of the dough lightly all over by hand. With the longest side closest to you, fold one third of the dough over the next third. Take the other third and fold it over the other two. You should have one long rectangle with three layers. Cut it into 4 equal pieces—you should have 4 rectangles.

continued on the next page ➡

SERVES: 4   ACTIVE TIME: 1 HOUR 30 MINUTES   TOTAL TIME: 2 HOURS 30 MINUTES

Take each rectangle and cut it into 6 equal strips. You should treat 6 strips as one ting momo now. Separate them out into 6 individual sections. Place 3 strips on the other 3 strips. Do the same with the rest. You should end up with 4 piles of stacked strips.

Hold the strips at the ends and pinch together, all the time pulling and stretching gently. Give them a twist a few times and twirl as if you were wringing out a towel by the ends. Now twist the whole thing in your hands to create a neat swirl. Tuck in the ends at the bottom and pop into the steamer. Do the same with the other 3 piles of strips and let rise for 30 minutes, covered, in a warm place.

Give the cabbage a stir—it should have wilted significantly by now. Add the texturized vegetable protein and the turmeric, give it all another stir, and let cook for a bit longer while the momos are rising. The cabbage lends itself to long, slow cooking—the longer you cook cabbage the tastier it gets—so just leave it on low heat with a lid on the pan.

Meanwhile, cut out 4 squares of parchment paper measuring 4 x 4 inches/10 x 10cm. When the momos have doubled in size, bring the water under the steamer to a boil. Place the momos on parchment paper squares in the steamer and steam for 12 minutes—no longer.

Dish up and eat while still warm. The cabbage should be lovely and soft, and because of the long cooking it will have bits that have caught and fried a little more than the rest—those are the best bits.

To eat, take a momo, peel away long pieces and use them to pick up the cabbage.

This is a double batch, so one half of the cabbage needs to be cooled completely. Once cool, put it into a bag and freeze.

photos of the finished dish on the next page ➻

Shawarmas are like the kebabs that you can justify as being good for you. Well, they're not particularly bad for you, really, and they are actually quite easy to make. You don't need a rotisserie or a special bread knife or pan. Let me show you how.

CHICKEN SHAWARMA

FOR THE SHAWARMA

2 tablespoons cornstarch

1 tablespoon salt

1 teaspoon ground cumin

1 teaspoon dried cilantro

1 teaspoon paprika

1 teaspoon ground turmeric

½ teaspoon ground cloves

1 tablespoon cayenne

1 teaspoon ground cinnamon

2 tablespoons vegetable oil

1 lb 10 oz boneless chicken thighs, halved

FOR THE SLAW

1 large head of broccoli, cut into florets

1¼ cups Greek yogurt

¼ cup vegetable oil

1 teaspoon mustard powder

1 tablespoon mustard seeds

1 teaspoon salt

fresh parsley, finely chopped

TO SERVE

flatbreads or pitas

Preheat the oven to 350°F/180°C and lightly grease a 9 x 5-inch/900g loaf pan.

For the shawarma, mix together the cornstarch, salt, cumin, dried cilantro, paprika, turmeric, cloves, cayenne, and cinnamon.

Put the oil into a bowl, then add the chicken and stir it around. Add the dry spice mix and stir to coat all the chicken pieces well. Layer the pieces of chicken in the loaf pan and press down, then bake in the oven for 40 minutes.

Meanwhile, make the slaw. Put the broccoli into a large bowl.

Put the yogurt into a second bowl. Heat the oil in a small pan. As soon as the oil is hot, add the mustard powder and seeds—when the seeds begin to pop, pour the oil and seeds over the yogurt, add the salt, and stir. Pour this dressing over the broccoli, then mix in the parsley.

When the shawarma is ready, let it rest in the pan for 10 minutes so that all the juices can go back into the chicken.

Tip the chicken out of the pan and slice your shawarma. We like to eat this piled into flatbreads with the slaw. Any leftovers can be kept in the fridge, or frozen for the next time you need your shawarma fix.

SERVES: 4   ACTIVE TIME: 20 MINUTES   TOTAL TIME: 1 HOUR

I never understood what was meant by tandoori chicken, until I realized it was the type of oven—a tandoor—they were talking about. So I have made the same dish my dad used to serve up in his restaurant, but using our oven at home. It has a similar red hue, but not so red that you'll question whether you will ever sleep again! It's served with an onion salad and browned butter rice.

"TANDOORI" OVEN CHICKEN WITH BROWNED BUTTER RICE

FOR THE CHICKEN

4 skinless chicken thighs and
　4 skinless breasts, flesh slashed

2 tablespoons ghee, melted

¼ cup tandoori spice mix
　(see p. 238)

FOR THE SAUCE

1⅔ cups yogurt

5 tablespoons chickpea flour

2 tablespoons melted ghee

¼ cup tomato paste

3 tablespoons tandoori spice
　mix (see p. 238)

FOR THE RICE

2½ cups basmati rice, rinsed
　and drained

¾ cup plus 2 tablespoons butter

1 teaspoon salt

1 quart boiling water

FOR THE SALAD

2 red onions, thinly sliced

2 green apples, cut into thin sticks

a squeeze of lemon juice

1 teaspoon salt

a small handful of fresh mint

TO SERVE

sliced red chiles, to taste

fresh cilantro, chopped

Preheat the oven to 425°F/220°C and have a roasting dish ready that all the chicken will fit into.

Put the chicken into the dish. Massage the ghee into the meat and sprinkle with the tandoori spice mix. Then bake in the oven for 15 minutes.

To make the sauce, put the yogurt, chickpea flour, ghee, tomato paste, and tandoori spice mix into a bowl and combine.

Lower the oven temperature to 400°F/200°C. Take the chicken out of the oven and pour the yogurt mix all over the top, then put back into the oven for 30 minutes.

Meanwhile, cook the rice. Put the butter into a large pan on high heat until it becomes golden brown. As soon as it does, add the rice and salt and stir. Add the hot water and keep stirring until it comes to a boil—when it does, keep stirring until all the liquid has evaporated. Pop the lid on the pan and let the rice steam on low heat for 10 minutes.

To make the salad, mix together the onions, apples, lemon juice, salt, and mint.

When the chicken is ready, sprinkle with red chiles and cilantro and serve with the browned butter rice.

SERVES: 8   TOTAL TIME: 45 MINUTES

This squash is cooked whole, with slits cut into it so all the flavor can permeate through. It's served with a simple burned garlic rice. Sometimes all we want is something hearty with veg, and that is exactly what this is.

HASSELBACK SQUASH WITH BURNT GARLIC RICE

FOR THE SQUASH

1 medium butternut squash

5 tablespoons vegetable oil

1 teaspoon salt

1 tablespoon ginger paste

1 teaspoon chile flakes

1 tablespoon dried rosemary

1 tablespoon ground cumin

1 lemon, finely grated zest
   and juice

fresh parsley, chopped,
   to finish

FOR THE RICE

3 tablespoons vegetable oil

7 tablespoons unsalted
   butter

1 whole head of garlic,
   peeled and sliced

2½ cups basmati rice

1 tablespoon salt

Preheat the oven to 400°F/200°C and have a roasting dish at the ready.

Peel your squash, then take off the top and bottom ends, cut it in half lengthwise, and scoop out the seedy bits. Now, with the cut side of the squash flat against the chopping board, make slits across it horizontally. Start at the top, working your way down and leaving ¼-inch gaps, ensuring each slit does not go all the way through the squash. Cut each half all the way through lengthwise, so you have 4 individual quarters. Don't worry if you accidentally cut too far when making the slits—just slide the pieces together when you put them in the roasting dish.

Put the oil, salt, ginger paste, chile flakes, rosemary, cumin, and zest and juice of the lemon into a bowl and mix together really well.

Put the squash in the roasting dish and smother it with the dressing. Bake in the oven for 30 minutes, until the squash is tender.

Meanwhile, cook the rice. Put the oil and butter into a large pot over medium heat. When the butter has melted, add the garlic and cook on high heat until it is almost black, stirring occasionally. As soon as it is very dark, take the pan off the heat and stir in the rice and salt.

Have a kettle of boiling water ready by your side. Cook the rice on medium heat for 3 minutes, or until the grains are an opaque white, stirring all the time. Pour in water until it is ½ inch above the level of the rice.

Cook the rice on high heat until all the water has been absorbed, stirring to make sure the rice doesn't stick to the bottom of the pot. Then turn the heat right down to the lowest setting, pop the lid on, and let the rice steam for 15 minutes.

Serve everyone some squash and rice, and sprinkle with the fresh parsley. You might like to add some Avocado Pesto (p. 27) to this, or the dressing from the Sweet Potato and Goat Cheese Tart (p. 110).

Any leftover rice can be frozen.

SERVES: 4   ACTIVE TIME: 30 MINUTES   TOTAL TIME: 1 HOUR

DESSERTS

This doesn't have to be made ahead, as it's so easy to whip together, but if you have any left over, just pop it into the freezer for another time. It's so simple it can be made with any fruit, but I like this combination, not to mention the beautiful color with flecks of minty green.

MANGO AND PEACH MINT SORBET

1 lb 2 oz frozen mango pieces

1 x 15-oz can of peaches, drained

¼ cup Greek yogurt

¼ cup golden syrup or light corn syrup

a small handful of fresh mint, chopped

Pop all the ingredients into a food processor and blitz until it comes together into a thick sorbet-type paste, making sure to occasionally scrape down the sides. If you find the mixture is not moving at any point, add an extra spoonful of yogurt.

While blitzing, you may find the sorbet becoming less frozen and more like a smoothie. If this is the case, pop it into the freezer for about 20 minutes before serving.

Store any leftovers in a Tupperware container, placed inside a ziplock bag to keep the sorbet soft and easy to scoop.

MANGO AND PEACH MINT SORBET FLOAT

You can serve any leftover sorbet as a drink: take a scoop of it and put it into the bottom of a glass. Add a few frozen berries if you have any in the freezer, then pour in some lemonade to make the perfect chilled tropical-flavored drink.

SERVES: 4   TOTAL TIME: 15 MINUTES

This is the simplest mousse, and we all need a quick mousse recipe for when we want dessert or something sweet. I for one love chocolate hazelnut spread, but I also love the spreads that used to be just chocolate bars and have been reborn as the same thing in jars in a spreadable form. You can use whichever you like.

CHOCOLATE HAZELNUT MOUSSE

⅔ cup chocolate hazelnut spread

3 tablespoons whole milk

2½ cups heavy cream

1 tablespoon cornstarch

3 tablespoons confectioners' sugar

⅔ cup roasted chopped hazelnuts, plus extra for sprinkling

whipped cream, from a can, to serve (optional)

cocoa powder for dusting, if you feel like it

Pop the chocolate hazelnut spread into a bowl with the milk and heat in the microwave in 10-second bursts until the mixture is runny and viscous but not steaming hot. This should not take more than 20 seconds. Set aside to cool.

Put the cream into a large bowl with the cornstarch and confectioners' sugar and begin whipping. As soon as it begins to thicken, pour in the chocolate mixture and keep whipping until you have stiff peaks.

Fold in the hazelnuts (keeping 1 tablespoon back for decorating), then spoon into a serving dish or individual ramekins. If you want it to look extra special, you can pipe the mousse in.

Serve with whipped cream, if desired, with an extra sprinkling of hazelnuts on top and a dusting of cocoa powder.

MAKES: 1 LARGE DISH OR 8 SMALL RAMEKINS   **TOTAL TIME:** 20 MINUTES

Does this even need an intro? S'mores are American madness in its best form: crunchy cookie, melted chocolate, and gooey marshmallow. They are not the easiest things to find here, so we often make them for the barbecue over the summer, but when we want a quick dessert this is the best thing ever! All made in a frying pan, with graham crackers to dive in.

FRYING PAN S'MORES

14 oz package of graham crackers

10½ oz dark chocolate, chips or cut into cubes, or choc of your choice

1 x 8-oz jar of salted caramel

40–45 medium marshmallows

For this you will need a frying pan or skillet that is safe to go into the oven, or alternatively, you can use a 9-inch round cake pan. I use either/or, whatever I have on hand.

Preheat the oven to 400°F/200°C and have the graham crackers ready. You want to eat these while they are still hot and oozy, so be prepared.

Layer the bottom with the cubes of chocolate, or chips if that is what you are using. Spread the caramel all over the top. This is not traditional; it's just an extra element I enjoy.

Carefully place the marshmallows on top, upright, and pack them in tightly. If you don't want to cook this straight away, it will be fine in the fridge until you're ready. Otherwise, bake in the oven for about 7 minutes.

It's ready when the marshmallows are golden brown and starting to puff up.

Time to dig in—take a graham cracker and dip it right into the bottom until you have melted chocolate, runny caramel, and stringy marshmallow on your crisp cookie.

Barfi is a delicious Indian sweet traditionally made with condensed milk and milk powder. It is my Abdal's absolute favorite. His eyes light up whenever someone opens up a box in front of him. But they take time and a little more effort to make your own, so this is my easy version. Everything goes into a processor and is blitzed, so if you are taking the appliance out of the cupboard, it's worth making double the amount. I like to eat them out of the fridge as little balls of energy, just perfect for when I need a sweet hit.

COCONUT BARFI TRUFFLES

⅓ cup pistachios

1 heaping cup dried apricots

5 cardamom pods, seeds removed from the pods and ground, or 1 teaspoon ground cardamom

1¾ cups dried shredded coconut, plus ¼ cup extra for coating

1 orange, finely grated zest only

up to 10 tablespoons condensed milk

Put the pistachios into the processor and blitz to crumbs. Add the apricots and blitz until they start falling apart.

Add the cardamom, coconut, and orange zest and blitz again to mix everything together.

With the motor running, slowly add the condensed milk—this is best done with the kind that comes in a squeezy bottle. Keep adding it until the mixture starts to clump together. When it does, it is ready to roll.

Have the extra coconut ready in a bowl. Take walnut-size mounds of the mixture and drop them into the coconut, roll them around to coat, then shape them into perfect balls.

Store them in an airtight container in the fridge. They can keep for up to a month, not that they last that long very often, but they're great for providing you with a regular sweet treat when you need one.

FLORENTINE COOKIES

Any leftover truffles can be made into Florentine cookies. Preheat the oven to 350°F/180°C and line a baking sheet with parchment paper. Place however many truffles you have left on the sheet, spacing them apart. With the base of a glass, squash each truffle so it is ¼ inch/6mm thick and bake for 8 minutes. Cool on a rack.

MAKES: ABOUT 25   TOTAL TIME: 30 MINUTES

Two of the things I always have in the house are chocolate bars and frozen puff pastry. For emergencies and for life in general. Put the two together and you have a pretty quick dessert—best of all, there is enough to make and put away for a rainy day.

CHOC BAR PUFFS

a little flour, for dusting

2 x 11-oz sheets of defrosted puff pastry

8 full-size chocolate bars, the kind that lend themselves to being melted, halved

1 egg, beaten

flaky sea salt (optional)

cocoa powder, for dusting

Dust your rolling pin with a little flour. Roll out one of the sheets of pastry, keeping it on the backing paper, and pop it onto a baking sheet. Have another baking sheet ready close by.

Place the bars evenly in line on the pastry, 5 across, 3 up, making sure to leave a good gap between the pieces of chocolate. There will be one extra—you're welcome, that's for you!

Take the second sheet of pastry and roll it out to ½ inch longer and wider than the other sheet. (This has to go over the chocolate, so it needs a bit more give.)

Brush all the edges of the first sheet of pastry around the chocolate with most of the egg. Now place the other piece of pastry on top. Using the side of your palm, press down gently around the cubes of chocolate to attach the top to the bottom. Once it is all sealed, pop it into the fridge for 5 minutes.

Preheat the oven to 400°F. Take the pastry off the sheet and cut out the little chocolate-filled cubes. Brush with the leftover egg. If you want a slightly more grown-up taste, you can sprinkle them with sea salt flakes. Divide them between the two sheets and pop them into the oven for 30 minutes, switching the sheets around halfway so they get an even bake and even golden-ness.

Once they are out of the oven, dust them with a little cocoa powder. If you are planning to freeze some, don't dust those with cocoa. Let them cool, then freeze in a freezer bag.

MAKES: 15   ACTIVE TIME: 10 MINUTES   TOTAL TIME: 40 MINUTES

These are so easy and quick, because there is no peeling of apples, no coring or chopping, so you can have your pie and eat it too. The filling is a mixture of applesauce mixed with spices, dried fruit, and nuts, then wrapped in filo, perfect enough to fit in the palm of your hand and in your mouth, in a bite, or two. They freeze well, so when you need pie, be it for yourself or for guests, you're always one step ahead.

APPLE PALM PIES

2 x 10-oz jars of chunky applesauce

½ teaspoon pumpkin pie spice

⅓ cup mixed nuts, or nuts of your choice, roughly chopped

⅓ cup raisins

cooking oil spray

10 oz package of filo pastry, or 6 sheets

Demerara sugar, for sprinkling

Put the applesauce, pumpkin pie spice, nuts, and raisins into a bowl, stir well, and set aside.

Preheat the oven to 400°F. Have a 12-hole muffin pan at the ready. Spray the inside of each hole liberally with oil.

Unroll the filo pastry onto a work surface. Stack all 6 sheets on top of each other and, using kitchen scissors, cut out all the pastry in one go to make 8 equal squares, which should give you 48 squares in total. Keep the squares you're not working with under a tea towel to prevent them drying out.

Take 1 square of filo and spray it with oil, lay another square on top, spray again, then lay another on top and spray again. You should have three squares oiled together. It doesn't matter if the squares are a bit off-center. Place inside an oiled cavity of the muffin pan, press down, and repeat this process until you have filled all 12 holes in the muffin pan.

Fill each hole with an equal amount of the apple filling.

Take another square of filo and spray well, then fold in half and in half again to create a small square. Place the small square on top of the apple mixture and fold the pointy edges inward. If any areas feel dry, spray with oil. Repeat for all 12, then sprinkle with sugar and bake for 14 to 16 minutes.

Let cool in the pan for 10 minutes. These are best eaten warm, with ice cream or custard.

Any leftover pies can be cooled and frozen. I know 12 wouldn't last very long in my household, so due to the ease of making these, why not double the ingredients and make another full 12 to freeze, providing you have freezer space!

Shrikand is a traditional Gujarati dessert made with a base of strained yogurt that's flavored, so sometimes when I want a lighter dessert this is great—and I have a way of making two desserts into one with this. Yogurt has the ability to take on flavor, so you could go wild and do all sorts. I love the aroma of traditional flavors and scents. With this recipe you'll make a batch of ice cream for later too—but if you'd prefer to just make the dessert for today, simply halve all ingredients.

SAFFRON ROSE SHRIKAND

FOR THE SHRIKAND

3½ cups Greek yogurt

1 tablespoon whole milk

10 strands of saffron

2½ cups heavy cream

6 tablespoons confectioners' sugar

1 teaspoon cornstarch

5 drops of rose extract/essence

TO SERVE

shortbread or brandy snaps

pistachios and rose petals

Start by straining the yogurt. Spoon the yogurt into a fine-mesh sieve set over a bowl or into a cheesecloth-lined colander. Set aside.

Heat the milk in the microwave, then add the strands of saffron and allow the color to bleed. The warmer the milk the stronger the color, so get it as warm as you can, which should only take a few seconds.

Put the cream into a bowl with the confectioners' sugar and cornstarch and whisk until you have soft peaks. This is not traditional, but I like to add the cream to make it a tiny bit richer, and the cornstarch helps to stabilize the cream. Be sure not to clear away the beaters, as you will need them again in a few minutes.

Add the strained yogurt to the whipped cream and fold in the saffron-infused milk. Once it is all an even golden color, stir in the rose extract.

Serve in small dishes with shortbread, or in brandy snaps (a thin tubular cookie popular in the UK), which is my personal favorite choice, and sprinkle with pistachios and rose petals. Do the same with the ice cream when you serve it.

SHRIKAND ICE CREAM

If you made the full batch, take half of the mixture and put it into another bowl, with ¼ cup of golden syrup or light corn syrup. This is an excuse to make shrikand ice cream: Simply whisk the syrup in and transfer to a freezer-safe Tupperware container. Pop the ice cream tub inside a ziplock bag and put it into the freezer. Shrikand for now, ice cream for later.

SERVES: 6   TOTAL TIME: 30 MINUTES

This is one of those cakes that looks suspiciously boring, plain even, but the three citrus fruits really pack it with a zing. It's simple and easy to make, and as it bakes it creates a delicious curd-like sauce that sits at the bottom, so there's no slicing—it's spoons in and serve. I like it with a little cream poured over the top, because there is always room for more sauce.

SAUCY CITRUS PUDDING

cooking oil spray

3 large eggs, separated

¼ cup/50g unsalted butter, melted

1 cup/200g granulated sugar

1 lemon, 1 lime, 1 small orange: finely grated zest of all 3, plus enough juice from all 3 to make 7 tablespoons/100ml (if you don't have enough, just use lemon or lime juice out of a bottle to top it up)

6 tablespoons/50g all-purpose flour

1 cup/240ml whole milk

confectioners' sugar, for dusting (optional)

heavy cream, to serve (optional)

Preheat the oven to 325°F/160°C and lightly spray the inside of an 8-inch/20cm square baking dish or medium casserole dish with oil.

Put the egg whites into a bowl big enough to whisk them in. Put the butter, sugar, zest and juice, egg yolks, flour, and milk into a second bowl.

Using a handheld mixer, whisk the egg whites until they are firm, meaning that the peaks will hold but the tips will fold back on themselves.

Take the same mixer and whisk the ingredients in the other bowl until you have a smooth, shiny cake batter.

Now add the whisked whites to the batter and fold them in until there are no foamy white bits left. Pour into the dish and bake for 45 minutes. Before serving, you can dust the top with confectioners' sugar if you like. Eat while it's still piping hot, topped with cream, if desired.

When you see a swirl in a dessert it looks like so much effort has been made, when in reality it's actually quite easy, especially in this case because the cake itself takes less time to bake than I do to get into bed. It's such a simple recipe—chocolate cake, creamy chocolate filling, all with a hint of lime. Chocolate limes used to be my fave sweets and I still can't resist them when I see them. You can use any jam you have left over at home, but I like lime marmalade—just for recipes like this, though; I'm not such a fan of it on my toast. I've given quantities for the ganache that will give you some extra chocolatey treats, but just halve the ingredients in **bold** if you only want to make the roulade today.

CHOC LIME ROULADE

FOR THE CAKE

3 large eggs

½ cup/100g sugar, plus extra for dusting

⅔ cup/75g all-purpose flour

⅓ cup/25g cocoa powder

FOR THE GANACHE FILLING

10½ oz/300g dark chocolate, chips or roughly chopped

7 tablespoons/100ml boiling water

10½ oz/300g cream cheese

¼ cup/80g lime marmalade

1 lime, finely grated zest only (save the rest of it)

Preheat the oven to 325°F/160°C, and grease and line a 9 x 13-inch/ 23 x 33cm baking dish with parchment paper.

Put the eggs and sugar into a bowl and whisk until the mixture has tripled in size and, when the beaters are lifted, leaves ribbons of egg on the surface. This will take up to 5 minutes.

Sift in the flour and cocoa and use a metal spoon to gently bring the mixture together. Keep mixing gently until there is no flour left in the bottom of the bowl.

Pour the mixture into the prepared baking dish and gently tilt it to encourage the mixture to get into the corners. When it has run as much as possible, carefully, without squashing the air bubbles out of the mixture, use a small spatula to guide the rest so that it covers the pan evenly.

Bake for 12 to 15 minutes.

Meanwhile, take a large sheet of parchment paper the same size as the cake and sprinkle it generously with sugar. As soon as the cake is baked, tip it upside down straight onto the waiting sugared paper and peel off the lining paper that it was baked on.

Now, with the long edge closest to you, roll up the whole thing, making sure to wrap it with the sugared paper encased in the roll. Let cool in the paper on a cooling rack.

continued on the next page ➡

SERVES: 6–8   TOTAL TIME: 1 HOUR 20 MINUTES

To make the ganache, put the chocolate into a bowl and microwave in bursts of 10 seconds until you have just a few unmelted pieces of chocolate. Now stir the chocolate—the heat of the bowl will help melt it—until smooth. Pour the boiling water a little bit at a time into the chocolate. Don't be alarmed—at first the chocolate will thicken as you stir. Just add a little more water and stir again. Repeat until you have a loose and glossy ganache.

Divide the ganache mixture in half. Set one half aside and add the cream cheese to the other half, whisking well until you have a creamy mixture.

Once the cake has almost cooled, unroll it and remove the parchment paper. Spread the cake with a thin layer of lime marmalade, then sprinkle with the zest. (Keep the lime, hollow it out, and fill the cavity with baking soda. If you place it in the back of your fridge, it will keep everything smelling fresh.)

Now spread a thin layer of the chocolate cream over the cake. Then, as you did before, roll the cake as it was until you get to the end. Make sure to place the roll seam-side down.

Drizzle with some of the remaining ganache, if you like, or see below for a suggestion on how to use it.

TRUFFLES

Put the leftover ganache into the fridge for at least 1 hour, until it's firm. When set, take small spoonfuls of the stuff, roll them into balls, then roll them in cocoa powder. Store them in the fridge so you can get a chocolatey treat every time you open the fridge door.

The ganache can be saved and turned into delicious truffles. These chocolatey treats are great to make with children on rainy days, and freeze brilliantly.

These are like doughnut meets cake meets fritter meets pakora. They are as fun to eat as they are to make. Crisp and sweet, and easy to demolish the lot. Apart from eating them, there is so much fun in squeezing the batter into the oil and being quick enough to create something that resembles a holey doughnut. To save yourself time you could make the batter the night before and just do the frying when it's time to eat.

STRAWBERRY MILKSHAKE FUNNEL CAKE

vegetable oil, for frying

2²/₃ cups/335g all-purpose flour

a pinch of salt

2 tablespoons confectioners' sugar

2 tablespoons baking powder

1 cup plus 2 tablespoons/275ml whole milk

2 large eggs

1 cup/100g strawberry-flavor powder

Start by heating some oil gently in a small pot, just big enough to fry one cake at a time. The oil should come halfway up the sides. I do these in a small pot so that I don't use up too much oil every time I fry.

Put the flour, salt, confectioners' sugar, baking powder, milk, and eggs into a bowl and whisk until you have a smooth batter.

Now there are a few ways of making these: You can place all the mixture in a ziplock bag and snip about ¼ inch/5mm off the end. Or you can use a squeezy bottle, although you don't want to squirt anything quickly into oil. I prefer to use a ziplock bag, and when I need to put it down, I just use a bag clip to stop the flow.

In one smooth motion, squeeze out the mixture in rounds, making sure that the batter connects to itself so it has something to hold on to. It should look like a spindly doughnut. Fry for roughly 1 minute on each side, or until golden brown. Have a baking sheet lined with paper towels at the ready, to drain the funnel cakes. As soon as they come out of the hot oil, sprinkle them generously with the strawberry powder and get to frying the next one.

HANDY TIP

These freeze really well, so if you have any left over, pop them into a freezer bag.

MAKES: ABOUT 20   TOTAL TIME: 30 MINUTES

These are like little molten chocolate cakes, the ones everyone says are notoriously difficult to make. They have a gingerbread cookie outer casing with a melty ganache in the center. They're fun to make and even more fun to eat. This recipe will give you 6 cakes to bake now, and another 6 to keep in the freezer for another time.

GINGERBREAD MELT-IN-THE-MIDDLES

FOR THE COOKIES

3⅔ cups/450g all-purpose flour

1 teaspoon baking soda

3 tablespoons ground ginger

½ cup plus 1 tablespoon/ 125g unsalted butter

¾ cup plus 1 tablespoon/ 175g brown sugar

¼ cup/60ml golden syrup or light corn syrup

1 large egg, beaten

FOR THE FILLING

7 oz/200g dark chocolate (or milk chocolate if you don't like dark, or white chocolate if you prefer it sweeter), chopped

¾ cup plus 2 tablespoons/ 200ml boiling water

a pinch of salt

¼ cup/40g crystallized ginger, very finely chopped

Mix together the flour, baking soda, and ground ginger in a bowl.

In a small pot melt the butter and sugar with the golden syrup. As soon as the sugar has melted, take off the heat and allow to cool for 5 minutes. Stir the beaten egg into the butter mixture and then add to the dry mix.

Bring the mix together until you have a smooth dough. Take away one third of the dough, wrap it in plastic wrap, and chill in the fridge. Form the bigger piece of dough into a sausage shape, then divide it into 12 equal balls.

Lightly grease the inside of a 12-cup muffin pan. Drop a ball of dough into each cavity and mold the dough so it is level on the bottom and sides and comes right to the top. Place in the fridge to chill.

To make the ganache, put the chopped chocolate into a bowl, pour in the boiling water, and stir until you have a smooth mixture. Sprinkle in the salt and the crystallized ginger, and let cool. As soon as it is cool, add some ganache to each cookie cavity, leaving a ½-inch/1cm gap at the top.

Place in the fridge to chill. Meanwhile, take out the remaining piece of dough and unwrap it. Roll it out, then cut out circles big enough to cover the top of the cakes. Pop a circle on each one, and be sure to pinch the edges to seal in that center. Freeze for 1 hour.

Preheat the oven to 350°F/180°C. Take the cakes out of the freezer, then pop 6 of them into a bag and return them to the freezer for later. Bake the remaining 6 for 25 to 27 minutes. Serve hot.

Bake the rest of the cakes from frozen at 350°F/180°C for 30 to 35 minutes. Be sure to bake them in the same muffin pan, as this will help them retain their shape.

I have this guy who knows everything there is to know about London—born and bred there, he could give Danny Dyer a run for his money, but for the most part I haven't a clue what he says. Between words I understand and the cockney rhyming slang, I tend to nod, unsure, and he laughs at me. This isn't really a cheesecake, but it tastes pretty good—more like lamington meets pasty. Once you feast your mince pies on these, you won't stop stuffing them into your north and south.

LONDON CHEESECAKE

2 sheets of defrosted
  puff pastry

6 tablespoons/120g
  strawberry jam, no lumps

1 egg yolk, lightly beaten

2 cups/250g confectioners'
  sugar

a few teaspoons of
  whole milk

½ cup/50g dried shredded
  coconut

Preheat the oven to 400°F/200°C. Line a baking sheet with parchment paper.

Unroll the two sheets of pastry and cut each one into 6 equal squares. Pop 6 of the squares onto the tray. Add 1 tablespoon of jam to the center of each one, avoiding the edges.

Brush lightly around the edge of each square with the egg yolk, then place another square of pastry on top and gently press the edges together. No crimping required. Every one of these that I have bought and eaten has tall sides and no crimping.

Pop them into the fridge for 10 minutes, then bake for 20 to 25 minutes, until the pastry is golden and puffy.

Let cool on a baking rack. As soon as they are totally cool, mix the confectioners' sugar with 1 teaspoon of milk at a time, until you have a thick icing. Spread the icing all over the top and sprinkle with the coconut immediately, while the icing is still wet.

These look bigger than your belly can eat, but they are light enough to finish. However, if you do have any left over that you haven't iced, you can freeze them.

SERVES: 6   ACTIVE TIME: 30 MINUTES   TOTAL TIME: 1 HOUR 15 MINUTES

Tiramisu is coffee, this is not! I don't know what else is left to say. So many will disagree, but go on, give it a little go. This is a great dessert to make ahead, and it will happily rest in the fridge overnight until you're ready to serve it.

GRAPEFRUIT TIRAMISU

3 large eggs, separated

¼ cup sugar

1 cup plus 2 tablespoons mascarpone

1 teaspoon vanilla bean paste

2 grapefruits, finely grated zest and ½ cup plus 2 tablespoons of juice

25–30 ladyfinger cookies

1 tablespoon cocoa powder, for dusting

Have a 1 quart or larger dish at the ready.

Put the egg yolks and sugar into a bowl and whisk until light and mousse-like. It should be pale and fluffy.

Put the mascarpone and vanilla into another bowl and beat until it's just a bit smoother. Add the egg yolk mixture and whisk until smooth.

Whisk the egg whites to stiff peaks. Then add them to the bowl a little at a time, folding gently with each addition.

Mix the grapefruit juice and zest in a bowl. Using 12 of the ladyfingers, dip each one quickly into the juice and arrange in the bottom of your dish. Pour half of the mascarpone over the top.

Do the same with the next 12 ladyfingers, layering them over the mascarpone. You may need to use a few more, depending on the size of your dish. If there is any extra juice and zest, pour it on top of the ladyfingers. Top with the rest of the mascarpone and smooth the surface.

Dust with the cocoa and chill in the fridge for at least 4 hours before serving, but ideally overnight.

I never really ate rice as a child, apart from boiled white rice, with curry, or pilau with curry. It was our thing, our staple, as people call it. So eating rice any other way never came to mind. But it turns out I can eat rice any which way, for which I am very grateful. Risotto, delicious—but sweet risotto, double delicious. If my rice farmer granddad were still alive, he would be proud. This recipe gives you a dessert today, with some leftover baked arancini balls for another day. If you'd rather not make those this time, simply halve all ingredients.

SWEET RISOTTO

1½ quarts whole milk

2½ cups heavy cream

1 tablespoon vanilla bean paste, or a whole vanilla bean, split

7 tablespoons unsalted butter

1 bay leaf

1 stick of cinnamon

3 cups risotto rice (such as Arborio)

1 teaspoon salt

¾ cup sugar

pulp from 8 passion fruits

Put the milk and cream into a pot, bring just to a boil, then lower the heat and cook on very low. If you are using a vanilla pod, pop it into the milk and cream while they are warming.

Heat the butter in a separate large nonstick pot, and as soon as it has melted, add the bay leaf and cinnamon stick and let them sizzle for 1 minute. Add all the rice and give it a good stir on medium heat, making sure to move it around all the time. This should take about 5 minutes—you will see the rice starting to change in appearance, the grains looking whiter.

Have a ladle ready and start adding 1 ladleful of the milk mixture at a time. As soon as some of it has evaporated, add some more, and keep doing this until there is no milk left. This can take a good 20 to 30 minutes.

Once the milk is finished and you have a thick risotto, take off the heat and stir in the salt, sugar, and vanilla bean paste, if using. Take out the bay leaf and cinnamon stick.

Put half the mixture into a dish and let cool. Eat the other half with the passion fruit pulp drizzled on top.

Refrigerate the cooled rice overnight. The next day, you can make it into sweet arancini balls. See opposite for how to make these.

SERVES: 6+   TOTAL TIME: 1 HOUR

SWEET ARANCINI BALLS

Crack 2 large eggs into a bowl and lightly whisk. Put ⅔ cup of breadcrumbs on a plate. Take tablespoons of the cold rice mix and make golf ball-size balls, using wet hands. If you happen to have an ice cream scoop, this is a good way to measure equal amounts of rice.

Dip the balls into the egg, then roll in the breadcrumbs and pop them onto a tray. Put them back into the fridge while you heat about 2 cups of vegetable oil in a pot small enough so you can cook just 2 arancini at a time. The oil should come just halfway up the pot. You'll know when the oil is hot enough if you drop in a bit of bread and it sizzles and floats. Carefully drop a rice ball in and fry until the outside is golden. Drain on paper towels and serve hot. You can warm some jam and use that as a dipping sauce, or sprinkle them with cinnamon sugar. If you have any sweet arancini balls left over, they can be frozen.

The best kinds of cookies are the ones that are homemade, but when I'm short on time, just divvying them up puts me off. So, I have found a way of making my cookie—cookie being the operative word—and eating it too. It's all made in one pan and cooked slowly on the stovetop till you have a lovely crust but a gooey center. I always think if you're going to make a cookie mixture, you might as well double it up and have some in the freezer, ready to bake. Simply double all the ingredients if you want to do this.

CHOC CHIP PAN COOKIE

½ cup plus 2 tablespoons/ 150g unsalted butter

¾ cup/160g brown sugar

1 large egg

½ teaspoon vanilla extract

½ teaspoon almond extract

1¾ cups/225g all-purpose flour

½ teaspoon baking soda

½ teaspoon salt

1 cup plus 2 tablespoons/ 100g chocolate chips or mini multicolored sugar-coated chocolates

Place a small nonstick, heavy-bottomed frying pan, about 9 inches/23cm, on medium to low heat. Add the butter and allow it to melt, then add the sugar and stir until it has dissolved. Take off the heat and let it cool for a few minutes.

While it's cooling, lightly beat the egg and add the vanilla and almond extracts.

Now add the flour, baking soda, and salt to the mixture in the frying pan, followed by the egg mix. Stir until you have a smooth cookie batter.

Press the batter down and sprinkle with the chocolate chips. Now cook on low heat for 15 to 20 minutes. If you find the bottom sticks, you may find it helpful to pop a lid on the pan for 5 minutes. What you should end up with is a crisp bottom and a gooey top.

Let it cool and set for about 15 minutes before you start eating. I like to take out slices and eat them hot with ice cream.

HANDY TIP

If you have made a double batch of batter, halve it before cooking, then roll this batch into walnut-size balls, place on a baking sheet lined with parchment paper, and pop in the freezer. Once frozen, transfer to a labeled freezer bag.

When you want to bake, preheat the oven to 325°F/160°C, pop the frozen cookies on a lined baking sheet, and bake for 20 to 25 minutes. Let cool on the sheet for 10 minutes before eating.

These are like scones, but not; they are like Welsh cakes, but not those either. They are a weird hybrid of the two that I like to fill with pecans and top with salted caramel and coffee cream. I always make enough to reserve half of these rounds, so I can pop them into freezer bags for another occasion.

PECAN ROUNDS WITH COFFEE CREAM

FOR THE ROUNDS

3⅔ cups/450g all-purpose flour

¾ cup plus 2 tablespoons/170g sugar

½ teaspoon salt

1 teaspoon baking powder

7 tablespoons/100g unsalted butter, chilled, plus 7 tablespoons/100g unsalted butter, melted for brushing

1 cup/100g pecans, finely chopped

2 large eggs, beaten

FOR THE COFFEE CREAM

2 tablespoons instant coffee

1 tablespoon hot water

1¼ cups/300ml heavy cream

2 tablespoons sugar

TO SERVE

salted caramel

Start by making the pecan rounds. Preheat the oven to 350°F/180°C. Grease two baking sheets and line with parchment paper.

Put the flour, sugar, salt, baking powder, and chilled butter into a bowl, and rub in the butter until you have breadcrumbs. Stir in the pecans.

Make a well in the center and add the eggs, then use a spatula to bring the dough together. Add a little water, 1 tablespoon at a time, until the dough just holds together. Roll it out on a floured surface to a thickness of ½ inch/1cm, and cut out rounds using a 2½-inch/6cm cutter. Collect the scraps and keep re-rolling and cutting until you have used up all the dough.

Brush the parchment paper on the baking sheets with melted butter. Place the rounds on the sheets with small gaps between them and brush again with butter. Bake for 20 minutes, then take them out and let them cool on a rack.

Add the coffee to the hot water and allow it to cool completely. Whisk the cream and sugar to soft peaks, then add the cooled coffee mixture and whisk it in quickly.

To serve, slather some salted caramel over the rounds and spoon on some of the coffee cream.

Whatever does not get eaten can be frozen.

MAKES: APPROX. 32   ACTIVE TIME: 40 MINUTES   TOTAL TIME: 1 HOUR

This cake combines salty, sweet, and zesty flavors. It's an assault on the senses but in a good way. Something a little different, but not steering too far away from the classics. While you're making up the batter, you might like to make an extra cake for the freezer—so just double up the cake ingredients if so.

PRESERVED LEMON SHEET CAKE

FOR THE CAKE

1 cup/225g unsalted butter, softened

1 cup plus 2 tablespoons/ 225g sugar

2½ cups/315g all-purpose flour, sifted

4¾ teaspoons baking powder

4 large eggs

¼ cup/60ml whole milk

1 lemon, finely grated zest only

FOR THE TOPPING

1 large or 2 small preserved lemons

1 x 6-oz/170g can of evaporated milk

Preheat the oven to 325°F/160°C. Grease and line a 9 x 13-inch/23 x 33cm baking pan with parchment paper.

Put the butter, sugar, flour, baking powder, eggs, milk, and zest into a mixing bowl and mix on high speed for 2 minutes, until you have a smooth, shiny batter. Pour it into the prepared pan and level the top.

Bake in the oven for 35 to 40 minutes.

Discard any seeds from the preserved lemon, then blitz with the evaporated milk in a blender and strain through a fine-mesh sieve.

While the cake is still hot, spread the salty lemony milk all over it, so it can be absorbed. After 15 minutes, remove the cake from the pan and it is ready to slice. This can be eaten cold, but is best warm.

The cake freezes well—just wrap it in foil and then tightly in plastic wrap.

These taste like regular éclairs, but there isn't anything regular about how you make them. Once they're filled with raspberry ripple cream, you stick a stick in, freeze them, and then cover them in chocolate—ice pop meets dessert meets pastry. A guaranteed amazing dessert ready to go in your freezer.

RIPPLE ÉCLAIR POPS

FOR THE CHOUX

½ cup/120ml whole milk

½ cup/120ml water

½ cup/120g unsalted butter

1¼ cups/150g all-purpose flour, sifted

a pinch of salt

2 teaspoons granulated sugar

4 large eggs, beaten

FOR THE FILLING

2½ cups/600ml heavy cream

3 tablespoons golden syrup or light corn syrup

1 teaspoon vanilla extract

1¼ cups/150g raspberries, blended and strained

2 tablespoons confectioners' sugar

TO FINISH

18 ice pop sticks

1 lb 5 oz/600g dark chocolate, melted

¾ cup/100g roasted hazelnuts, chopped (optional)

Start by making the choux. Preheat the oven to 400°F/200°C and line two baking sheets with parchment paper, lightly greased.

Put the milk and water into a pot with the butter and bring to a boil. Take it off the heat, then add the flour, salt, and sugar in one go and beat vigorously until you have a smooth paste. Pop it back on the heat to cook the flour out for 2 minutes.

Take the pan off the heat again and transfer the dough to a bowl. Now add the eggs a little at a time. Keep mixing after each addition and it will come together. When all the eggs are used up, you should have a smooth, glossy paste. Pop it into a piping bag and snip off the corner to make a ½-inch/1.5cm hole.

Slowly pipe 4-inch/10cm lines of dough about 1 inch/2.5cm wide onto the baking sheets, leaving a 1-inch/2.5cm gap in between. Once you have done them all, lower the oven temperature to 350°F/180°C and bake them for 25 minutes, switching the position of the sheets halfway through.

Take them out of the oven (keep the oven on) and pierce a hole in the base of each with the back of a wooden spoon, then put them back into the oven, hole side up, to dry out. Take out after 5 minutes and let cool completely while you make the cream.

Whip the cream, golden syrup, and vanilla to soft peaks. Mix the strained raspberries with the confectioners' sugar and ripple through the cream. Pop the cream into a piping bag and start to fill each éclair through the little hole, until the piping bag gets pushed out. You may have to twist the tip about to try and get as much cream into it as possible.

Place the éclairs on a baking sheet quite close together and top with a layer of parchment paper. Pop a stick into the rounded end of each one and freeze. They will need at least 1 hour. Just before taking them out of the freezer, melt the chocolate. There are two ways of eating these. Dip and eat while the chocolate slowly sets. Or dip, then sprinkle with the nuts and freeze for another 1 hour.

If we can use ginger as a spice in cake, somewhere in my mind black pepper feels acceptable too. It's a subtly scented spice that works so well in a sticky cake like this. Try it, if only out of curiosity. This is another cake that you can make ahead and keep in the freezer or make a couple so you have one for now and one for later (double all the ingredients if you'd like to do this).

BLACK PEPPER CAKE

⅔ cups/75g all-purpose flour

2 heaped teaspoons ground black pepper

½ teaspoon baking soda

2 tablespoons whole milk

7 tablespoons/150g molasses

5 tablespoons/75g unsalted butter

⅓ cup/75g light brown sugar

5 tablespoons/75ml water

1 large egg, beaten

Preheat the oven to 325°F/170°C and line a 9 x 5-inch/900g loaf pan.

Sift the flour and pepper into a large bowl. Mix the baking soda and milk in a separate small bowl and set aside.

Heat the molasses, butter, sugar, and water in a pot until dissolved. Let it cool a bit, then add to the dry mix and mix to a smooth, shiny batter. Add the egg and mix in well, then stir in the milk and baking soda mixture.

Spoon into the loaf pan and bake for 1 hour, or until a skewer comes out clean.

Malai ice cream is a subtly scented milk-based ice cream that you can find in South Asia and often in the UK too. This is my no-churn version—it goes well with the sweet tatin, but will also go further, leaving enough for a few extra desserts.

BANANA TARTE TATIN WITH MALAI ICE CREAM

FOR THE ICE CREAM

1 x 14-oz/397g can of
condensed milk

2 cups/480ml heavy cream

5 cardamom pods, seeds
removed from the pods
and ground

FOR THE BANANA TARTE TATIN

1 x 17.3-oz/490g package of
puff pastry

½ cup/100g brown sugar

5 tablespoons/75g unsalted
butter

¼ cup/40g chopped
hazelnuts

4 or maybe 5 bananas, sliced
into ¾-inch/2cm coins

Make the ice cream first. Put the condensed milk, cream, and ground cardamom seeds into a bowl. Whip until thick and at soft-peak stage, then transfer to a freezer-safe tub and level the top. Place inside a ziplock bag and freeze.

Now on to the tarte tatin. Preheat the oven to 350°F/180°C and have a 9-inch/23cm round oven-safe pan at the ready.

If your puff pastry is divided into two sheets, brush one sheet with cool water and stick the two sheets together. Roll out the pastry to a circle about ¾ inch wider than your pan. Pop it on a baking sheet and chill it in the fridge while you make the caramel.

Put the sugar and butter into the pan, and place over medium heat. When the sugar dissolves, turn up the heat and allow the caramel to get dark and thicken. Lift the pan and give it all a little swirl occasionally. The main thing is to watch it until it is a deep caramel color, because once it gets to that point, it can burn quickly. Take off the heat and sprinkle with the hazelnuts.

Add the bananas to the caramel, then lay the pastry on top and gently lift and tuck it around the sides of the pan, being careful of the hot caramel. Cut a slit in the top for the steam to escape, and bake for 25 to 30 minutes.

Let it stand for at least 20 minutes after it comes out of the oven. Then turn it over onto a serving plate and serve with the ice cream.

From the moment I first made these cinnamon goodies, I have been addicted. They are delicious, and there is nothing better than incorporating warm cinnamon flavors into a cake. These can be cut into squares and frozen, so you don't have to eat them all at once unless you really want to.

SPECULOOS COOKIE SHEET CAKE

FOR THE CAKE

1 cup plus 2 tablespoons/ 250g unsalted butter, softened

1 cup plus 3 tablespoons/ 250g dark brown sugar

⅓ cup/100g Belgian speculoos cookie butter spread

½ teaspoon ground cinnamon

½ teaspoon salt

5 large eggs

2 cups plus 6 tablespoons/ 300g all-purpose flour, sifted

FOR THE TOPPING

7 oz/200g white chocolate

¾ cup plus 2 tablespoons/ 200ml heavy cream

5¼ oz/150g Belgian speculoos cookies, crushed

Preheat the oven to 325°F/170°C. Grease and line a 9 x 13-inch/23 x 33cm baking pan with parchment paper, leaving a bit of overhang on the long sides.

Put the butter and sugar into a mixing bowl and beat until the mixture is light and pale and fluffy. Add the cookie butter spread, cinnamon, and salt, and mix well.

Add the eggs one at a time, stirring each one in, then fold in the flour until you have an even, smooth, shiny batter. Spread it in the prepared pan and level the top.

Bake for 30 to 35 minutes, until a skewer inserted in the center comes out clean, then let cool completely in the pan.

Meanwhile, make the topping. Put the white chocolate into a bowl. Heat the cream in a pot until it just comes to a boil, then take off the heat and pour the cream over the chocolate. Let it sit for half a minute . . . don't be tempted to stir just yet. When the chocolate starts to melt, stir until the mixture is silky smooth.

Stir in the crushed cookies, then spread the topping all over the cooled cake. Once the topping has set, lift the cake out of the pan, using the paper to help you, and cut it into squares.

MAKES: 18 SQUARES   ACTIVE TIME: 40 MINUTES   TOTAL TIME: 2 HOURS

I had always imagined that baklava would be very sweet, like Indian sweets, and I wasn't wrong—it is sweet, but there's something about the crunchy, sticky pastry and nuts that makes you forget. This is my favorite combination of chocolate and orange, and I like to eat it the way we did in Turkey, with copious amounts of clotted cream on top.

CHOCOLATE AND ORANGE BLOSSOM BAKLAVA

3 cups/300g mixed nuts

3 tablespoons golden syrup or light corn syrup

½ teaspoon salt

2 tablespoons cocoa powder

1 orange, finely grated zest only (save the juice for the syrup)

¾ cup plus 2 tablespoons/ 200g unsalted butter

2 x 10-oz/270g packages of filo pastry, defrosted

2 x 5-oz/140g pots of clotted cream or 1¼ cups/300g crème fraîche, to serve

FOR THE SYRUP

1¼ cups/250g sugar

2 tablespoons honey

1 tablespoon orange blossom water

orange juice, freshly squeezed and topped off with water to make ¾ cup plus 2 tablespoons/200ml of liquid

4 cardamom pods, seeds removed and crushed

Preheat the oven to 325°F/160°C. Grease an 8-inch/20cm square cake pan.

In a food processor, blitz the nuts until ground to small, even pieces. Stir in the syrup, salt, cocoa powder, and orange zest and set aside.

Melt the butter, then open your first package of filo pastry. Cut the sheets in half so you have a pile of squares. Place your cake pan on top and trim the pastry with a sharp knife so it is the same size as the bottom of the pan.

Brush a square of pastry with butter and lay it in the bottom of the cake pan, then do the same to every single square until you have all that pastry inside the pan. Press the pastry down firmly every time you put in a square. Put the nuts on top and press down again to create an even layer.

Open the second package of pastry and, again, cut it in half and trim the edges to fit the pan. Layer each piece one on top of the other as before, brushing with melted butter and pressing down. If there's any butter left over, just pour it on top.

With the pastry still in the pan, use a sharp knife to cut out the squares, making sure to get all the way to the bottom layer. Bake for 20 minutes, then lower the heat to 275°F/130°C and bake for another 45 minutes.

To make the syrup, mix together the sugar, honey, orange blossom water, and juice. Add the crushed cardamom pods and let them infuse for a couple of minutes, then remove. Bring to a boil, then lower to a simmer for 10 minutes. Once the baklava is out of the oven, pour the syrup all over and let cool completely.

I like to decorate these with edible golden stars. They are best eaten with a smothering of clotted cream.

MAKES: 16   ACTIVE TIME: 40 MINUTES   TOTAL TIME: 2 HOURS

Sometimes when I want a quick dessert, I want to make some elements of it and buy the others—that makes me feel less like I've done nothing and better because I've done a little something, no matter how insignificant. I love hot and cold and texture, so this is my recipe for hot burnt butterscotch over room-temp store-bought rice pudding, with freezing cold ice cream. There is enough sauce here to either freeze for another time or make frappés (see below).

BURNT BUTTERSCOTCH BANANAS WITH ICE CREAM AND RICE PUDDING

1⅓ cups unsalted butter

2⅓ cups light brown sugar

2½ cups heavy cream

a pinch of salt

3 bananas, sliced

4 x 4-oz containers of rice pudding

vanilla ice cream

Put the butter into a medium nonstick pot and melt over medium heat. Keep the butter on the heat until it is foamy and golden brown, 4 to 5 minutes.

Stir in the sugar and the cream, then lower the heat and cook gently for 7 to 10 minutes, stirring continuously, until the mixture thickens. Add the salt.

Take off the heat and let cool for a bit. Don't forget this is boiling sugar, so be careful. Place half in a freezer-safe Tupperware container and set aside. Add the sliced bananas to the remaining sauce and mix well.

To serve, divide the rice pudding between your bowls, then pour on the burnt butterscotch and bananas and add a scoop of ice cream.

BURNT BUTTERSCOTCH FRAPPÉ

For the leftover butterscotch, frappé is all I'm saying. To make 2 drinks, take 2 large handfuls of ice cubes, ¼ cup butterscotch sauce, 7 table-spoons strong black coffee, and 1¼ cups whole milk.

Blend the lot in a blender and pour into glasses. Add some whipped cream straight out of a can and drizzle with a little more butter-scotch sauce.

SERVES: 4   TOTAL TIME: 30 MINUTES

So this is an actual thing, and I saw it when I was scrolling through social media. That last bit of milk at the bottom of the cereal bowl is the best—it has all the sugar and all the flavor—so it feels only right to turn it into an ice cream.

CEREAL MILK ICE CREAM

5 cups heavy cream

3⅔ cups Frosted Flakes cereal, plus extra for sprinkling

¾ cup plus 2 tablespoons condensed milk

5 tablespoons golden syrup or light corn syrup

Pour the cream into a large bowl, and add the cereal, condensed milk, and golden syrup. Stir well, making sure the cereal is submerged, then let sit for 1 hour or more in the fridge, to make sure the cream is cold enough to whip.

Strain the cereal out of the milk and pop it into another bowl. Don't forget to have a bowl underneath the sieve, or you'll lose that precious cream.

Whip the cream mixture to soft peaks.

Using the back of a fork, mash up the cereal just a little bit. Fold it into the cream mixture, using the fork to help separate the flakes of soggy cereal.

Pour into a freezer-safe, airtight container and sprinkle with some extra cereal to cover the top completely. Put the lid on, then pop into a large ziplock bag—this will ensure that you always have a soft scoop, as it will prevent the ice cream from hardening—and freeze for a minimum of 2 hours.

This cookie base is beautiful, with its dark black cocoa color contrasting with the pink panna cotta. Whenever I have panna cotta, I feel like it needs something crunchy to go with it, and this is exactly that in a tart. Another great dessert for making ahead, as you can just pop it in the fridge until you're ready to serve it chilled.

CHOCOLATE ROSE PANNA COTTA TART

FOR THE TART SHELL

24 chocolate sandwich
  cookies

6 tablespoons unsalted
  butter, melted

FOR THE GANACHE LAYER

3½ oz milk chocolate

7 tablespoons heavy cream

FOR THE ROSE
PANNA COTTA

¾ cup plus 2 tablespoons
  whole milk

1¼ cups heavy cream

2 tablespoons sugar

1 envelope (¼ oz/
  1 tablespoon) of powdered
  gelatin

1 teaspoon rose extract

a few drops of pink
  food coloring

Have a 10-inch fluted round tart pan with a removable bottom ready. Put the cookies into a food processor and blitz to fine crumbs. Mix in the butter, then transfer to the tart pan and spread all over the bottom and sides. Pop into the freezer for 15 minutes.

To make the ganache, put the chocolate into a bowl and microwave in bursts of 10 seconds, until you have just a few pieces of unmelted chocolate remaining. Now stir the chocolate—the heat from the bowl will help melt it—until smooth. Bring the heavy cream just to a boil in a small pot and pour it, a little at a time, into the chocolate. Don't be alarmed—at first the chocolate will thicken as you stir. Add another bit of cream and stir. Repeat this, stirring until you have a glossy mixture. Let cool.

Now get started on the panna cotta. Put the milk, cream, and sugar into a pot and sprinkle the powdered gelatin over the surface. Let stand for 5 to 10 minutes. Bring to a simmer, stirring until the gelatin dissolves, then turn off the heat. Add the rose extract and pink coloring, and let cool for 30 minutes.

In the meantime, pour the ganache into the tart pan and pop back into the freezer to set.

When the panna cotta is only warm to the touch, pour it into the tart pan and chill in the fridge for at least 2 hours before eating.

One day I want to go to Sweden and eat one of these, right on its own soil. I have made many of them, but this is a simplified one, using as many elements as possible from the cake without having to make the tricky marzipan dome. Same delicious taste, with a new look. (See p. 183 for a photo of the finished torte.)

PRINCESS TORTE CAKE

FOR THE CUSTARD

2½ cups/600ml whole milk

1 teaspoon vanilla bean paste

3 large egg yolks

½ cup plus 2 tablespoons/ 125g sugar

½ cup/50g cornstarch, plus extra for dusting

FOR THE CAKE

1¼ cups/250g sugar

8 large eggs

2 cups/250g all-purpose flour, sifted

TO FINISH

2 limes, finely grated zest only

a few drops of green food coloring

9 oz/250g white marzipan

¾ cup/250g raspberry jam

Start by making the custard so it has plenty of time to chill. Heat the milk and vanilla in a pot until it comes up to a simmer, then take the pan off the heat.

Put the egg yolks, sugar, and cornstarch into a bowl and whisk until the mixture is light and fluffy. This takes about 5 minutes. Slowly add the warm milk, whisking all the time, until all the milk has gone in. Pour the mixture back into the pot and mix slowly over low to medium heat until the custard becomes really thick. Take off the heat and transfer to a bowl. Give it a few minutes to cool, then cover and chill in the fridge.

Start the cake now. Preheat the oven to 325°F/160°C, and grease and line two 9-inch/23cm round cake pans. When you cut out the two rounds of paper for the base, cut out a third to use as a template for the marzipan.

Whisk the sugar and eggs in a mixer for 10 minutes on high speed, until the mixture has tripled in size. Fold the flour in gently with a large metal spoon, being careful not to knock out all that air.

Divide the mixture between the two pans and bake for 25 to 30 minutes.

While the cakes are baking, add the zest and the green coloring to the marzipan and knead it until you get an even color. Roll out and make a 9-inch/23cm circle, using your extra circle of parchment paper. Dust the surface with a little bit of cornstarch to prevent the marzipan from sticking, and pop it into the freezer to firm up a little.

Take the cakes out of the oven and cool on a wire rack. Slice each cake in half horizontally, and sandwich them back together with almost all of the raspberry jam.

Place one cake on your serving dish. Pop the custard into a piping bag and pipe kisses on top. Brush the top of the next cake with a tiny bit of jam to act as glue and lay the marzipan on top. Then place this cake on top of the custard.

When this cake isn't being eaten, it needs to be kept in the fridge. To serve, add a fresh rose on top.

SERVES: 8   ACTIVE TIME: 1 HOUR   TOTAL TIME: 2 HOURS 30 MINUTES

After my travels in Nepal last year, I became enamored with food in little parcels. I already love samosas, so it's no wonder I love these little parcels with sweet and savory fillings. I have made various versions of these, and this is one of my favorites. These are made with a chocolate pastry and filled with chocolate and nuts, with a quick raspberry sauce to go with them.

CHOCO MOMOS WITH RASPBERRY SAUCE

FOR THE PASTRY

1¾ cups/220g all-purpose flour, plus extra for dusting

⅓ cup/30g cocoa powder

2 tablespoons vegetable oil

a pinch of salt

boiling water

FOR THE FILLING

⅓ cup/100g chocolate hazelnut spread

1 cup/100g mixed nuts, finely chopped

FOR THE SAUCE

1¼ cups/150g raspberries, fresh or frozen

3 tablespoons confectioners' sugar

1 tablespoon lemon juice

Start by making the pastry. Put the flour into a bowl with the cocoa powder and mix well. Mix in the oil and salt, then make a well in the center and add boiling water a little at a time until the dough starts to come together. It will still be too floury at this point, and that's okay.

As soon as the dough is cool enough to handle, get your hands in and bring it together. If it's still too floury, add a little water, 1 tablespoon at a time, until all the dough is in one piece and there is no flour left. It should not be wet or tacky. Knead the dough for a few minutes on a work surface until it is smooth and shiny.

To make the filling, mix the chocolate hazelnut spread and nuts together. To make the sauce, blitz the raspberries, confectioners' sugar, and lemon juice together in a blender until smooth. I like to make it extra smooth by straining it through a fine-mesh sieve.

To make the momos, roll the dough out into a sausage shape about 16 inches/40cm long on a very lightly floured surface. Cut it into 20 equal pieces, then roll each piece into a disk about 4 inches/10cm in diameter. While you're rolling, cover the rest of the dough with a damp tea towel.

Add a small spoonful of filling to the center of each disk. There are various ways of sealing a momo, and there are tutorials online. But for a basic shape, just use your finger to brush a small amount of water around the edges, then simply bring the dough to the center and pinch to seal it tightly.

To cook these, they need steaming. You can freeze them at this point if you want. I have a steamer that sits on top of a pot of boiling water, but you can use an electric steamer, a bamboo steamer, or even a colander placed on top of a pot of boiling water with a lid that fits tightly.

Cut a small piece of parchment paper for each momo to sit on. Place the momos inside the steamer in batches and steam for 12 to 15 minutes. The pastry should puff out and become glossy. Once steamed, they are ready to be drizzled with the sauce.

Ras malai is Bengali for "juice creams." They are these little bits of cake that bob around in gently spiced milk, like a floating cheesecake thing. This is my version, without the floating. Same delicious flavors—rich, creamy, lightly spiced, and fragrant.

RAS MALAI CAKE

FOR THE CAKE

10 strands of saffron, dropped into ¼ cup/60ml of warm milk

1 cup plus 2 tablespoons/ 250g unsalted butter, softened

1¼ cups/250g granulated sugar

5 large eggs, beaten

2¼ cups/280g all-purpose flour

4¼ teaspoons baking powder

FOR THE MILK DRIZZLE

1½ cups/100g powdered milk

½ cup plus 2 tablespoons/ 150ml boiling water

3 cardamom pods, seeds removed from the pods and ground

FOR THE BUTTERCREAM

2 cardamom pods, crushed

3 tablespoons whole milk

1⅓ cups/300g unsalted butter, softened

4¾ cups/600g confectioners' sugar, sifted

TO DECORATE

edible rose petals, mixed with 1 cup/100g roughly chopped pistachios

Preheat the oven to 325°F/170°C. Grease and line two 8-inch/20cm round cake pans with parchment paper.

Make the saffron milk. Place the butter and sugar in a bowl and beat until light and fluffy and almost white. Add the eggs a little at a time, making sure to keep beating. Then add the flour, baking powder, and saffron milk, and fold the mixture until you have a smooth, shiny batter.

Divide the batter between the two pans and level the tops. Bake for 30 to 35 minutes.

Meanwhile, make the milk drizzle by pouring the boiling water over the powdered milk in a bowl and mixing well. Mix in the ground cardamom seeds, then strain through a fine-mesh sieve. As soon as the cakes are out of the oven, drizzle the milk all over the top of both cakes and let them cool in the pans for at least 10 minutes before turning them out and removing them to cool on a rack.

To make the buttercream, put the crushed cardamom pods in a small bowl with the milk and let infuse.

Meanwhile, put the butter into a mixing bowl and beat until very soft and light in color. Add the confectioners' sugar a little at a time, beating after each addition, until all combined. Then pour the cardamom milk through a fine-mesh sieve into the buttercream and beat until really light and fluffy.

Once the cakes are totally cool, place one cake on your serving dish and spread an even layer of buttercream over it. Put the other cake on top, flipping it over so the milk drizzle top becomes the bottom and sandwiches the buttercream. Spread some buttercream evenly across the top and the sides and use a ruler to level off the edges.

If you have any buttercream left over, you can pipe little kisses on top. Then gently take the rose petals and pistachios and press them into the sides of the cake.

SERVES: 8   ACTIVE TIME: 1 HOUR   TOTAL TIME: 2 HOURS

BASICS

DRY SPICE

MAKES: ABOUT 1 CUP/110g   **TOTAL TIME:** 5 MINUTES

12 lime leaves

2 nori sheets

2 tablespoons ground ginger

2 tablespoons granulated garlic

3 tablespoons granulated onion

3 tablespoons celery salt

1 teaspoon salt

2 tablespoons chile flakes

1 tablespoon white sesame seeds

1 tablespoon black sesame seeds (if you can't find these, you can just use the same amount of white)

2 teaspoons dried cilantro

This incredibly versatile, flavorful spice mix is perfect for marinades or to use as a rub on meats and vegetables. I often use this to make my super-quick version of instant noodles—cook 1½ oz noodles per person, and stir 1 teaspoon of this into it. Add 1 teaspoon of the spice paste from p. 78 too, if you like.

Grind the lime leaves and nori sheets to a fine powder. Place in a medium jar along with all the other ingredients. Put the lid on and shake to mix until it is all well incorporated.

BENGALI SPICE MIX (PANCH PHORAN)

MAKES: ABOUT 1 CUP/100g   **TOTAL TIME:** 5 MINUTES

3 tablespoons nigella seeds (or black sesame seeds or even poppy seeds)

3 tablespoons brown mustard seeds

3 tablespoons fennel seeds

3 tablespoons cumin seeds

3 tablespoons fenugreek seeds

You'll find this in my Corned Beef Bombay Pie (p. 118) and Watercress Quinoa Kedgeree (p. 119), but it's a great one to have in your cupboard all the time. It goes brilliantly with meat, fish, vegetables, and lentils. All you need are equal amounts of the five spices listed, so if you don't want to make a whole jar, simply decrease the quantities. It works well ground into pastries for added flavor, or simply cook it in some oil at the start of any stew or curry to add something a little bit special.

Grind all the ingredients together until fine, then transfer to a clean, dry jar to store.

THAI GREEN CURRY PASTE

MAKES: APPROX. 2 LB   **TOTAL TIME:** 25 MINUTES

½ cup plus 2 tablespoons/ 150ml vegetable oil

3 heads of garlic, peeled

9 oz ginger, peeled and chopped into chunks

1 medium onion, peeled and roughly chopped

3¼ oz lemongrass (6 sticks), fibrous outer layers removed

¼ oz package of lime leaves

3 limes, finely grated zest and juice

10 small green bird's-eye chiles

scant 1 oz cilantro, stalks and all

5 tablespoons fish sauce

1 tablespoon brown sugar

2 tablespoons salt

Yes, you can buy this in a shop, but the flavors are so much more powerful when you make your own.

Place all the ingredients into a blender and whiz till you have a smooth paste. This is enough for two decent-sized curries. The paste will differ in consistency depending on how juicy the limes are and how fresh the ginger is.

To make a curry, all it needs is either 14 oz of cooked jumbo shrimp, or 1 lb 2 oz of diced chicken breast if you prefer, with some green beans or veg of your choice and a 13.5-oz can of coconut milk.

It can be kept in the fridge for 6 weeks or in the freezer for 3 months.

TANDOORI SPICE MIX

MAKES: ABOUT 1 CUP/100G   **TOTAL TIME:** 5 MINUTES

1-oz jar ground ginger

1½-oz jar ground cumin

1¼-oz jar ground coriander

1½-oz jar paprika

1½-oz jar cayenne

1½ oz salt

2-oz jar granulated garlic

This recipe will make you a huge batch, but I use it in practically everything! You'll need it for the "Tandoori" Oven Chicken (see p. 178), but it's also a great addition to any marinade or curry. It's good rubbed into fish or chicken and works really well as a seasoning for potato wedges or burger patties.

Place all the ingredients in a large jar and shake well to combine.

MY FAVORITE CURRY PASTE

MAKES: APPROX. 2 LB   TOTAL TIME: 25 MINUTES

¾ cup plus 2 tablespoons/ 200ml vegetable oil, plus extra for cooking

7-oz jar of chopped garlic

7-oz jar of chopped ginger

3 tablespoons garam masala

1 lb 7 oz frozen chopped onions, defrosted

¼ cup chile powder (or paprika, if you prefer a milder curry)

2 teaspoons ground turmeric

3 tablespoons salt

¼ cup honey

¼ cup tomato paste

1 tablespoon tamarind paste or sauce

1 lemon, juice only

This is my favorite base for a curry. It packs loads of flavor and is so versatile. It works with meat or fish, or just any leftover veg you might have in the fridge.

Put all the ingredients in a food processor and blitz to a smooth paste. Pour 3 tablespoons of oil into a pot and heat. Scrape all the mixture from the food processor into the pot, and cook over medium heat, stirring frequently, for 20 minutes. The mixture will turn into a rich, dark paste. Once cooked, transfer to a clean jar and let cool completely before storing in the fridge. It will keep in the fridge for 1 month or in the freezer for 3 months.

PANCAKE BATTER

SERVES: 4   TOTAL TIME: 10 MINUTES

2 cups all-purpose flour

1 teaspoon baking powder

½ teaspoon salt

3 tablespoons sugar

¾ cup whole milk

2 large eggs

2 tablespoons vegetable oil

This is one of the quickest things you can whip up in the morning—it practically takes the same amount of time as pouring a bowl of cereal. And it's always a winner with the kids. Top with fruit and maple syrup—or use in the sheetpan pancake on p. 24. You can also prepare it in advance—in fact, batter is often better if it has rested—so make it the night before and after a quick stir in the morning, it will be ready to pour into a hot pan.

Make the batter by combining the flour, baking powder, salt, and sugar in a bowl. Whisk the dry ingredients together.

Make a well in the center and add the milk, along with the eggs and oil. Whisk it all until you have a thick, smooth batter.

To make pancakes, heat a nonstick frying pan over a medium heat. Add a knob of butter and swirl it around. Add a large spoonful of batter (or less, depending on what size pancake you'd like to make). Once a few bubbles start to appear on the surface, flip it over and cook for another minute or two, until both sides are golden. Serve hot with toppings of your choice.

GARLIC BREAD

MAKES: 12

TOTAL TIME: 2 HOURS 30 MINUTES   ACTIVE TIME: 30 MINUTES

3⅔ cups/450g all-purpose flour

1 package (2¼ teaspoons/7g) fast-acting instant yeast

1 teaspoon sugar

1 teaspoon salt

¼ cup/50g unsalted butter, plus more for greasing

1¼ cups/300ml warm water

2 tablespoons coarse semolina

5 tablespoons/75g butter, melted

5 cloves of garlic, grated

a small handful of fresh parsley, chopped

a good pinch of kosher salt or flaky salt

What meal isn't improved by garlic bread? It's especially lovely alongside my Mushroom Lasagne (p. 156) or Chorizo Fish Stew (p. 168).

Put the flour, yeast, sugar, and salt into a bowl. Add the butter and rub it in. Make a well in the center and add the water, then bring the dough together and knead for 10 minutes, until it is smooth and stretchy. Put it back into the bowl, cover, and let rise for 1 hour, or until the dough has doubled in size.

Have ready a roasting dish, lightly greased and with semolina sprinkled over the bottom. Knock the dough back into the bowl, then tip out onto a floured surface. Divide it into golfball-size pieces and put them in the dish, leaving small gaps in between to give the dough room to grow. Cover and let rise until doubled in size.

Preheat the oven to 325°F/160°C and bake the garlic bread for 40 to 45 minutes.

Meanwhile, combine the melted butter, garlic, parsley, and salt. As soon the rolls come out of the oven, brush all the butter on top of them.

Any leftovers can be frozen (you could also freeze the uncooked dough balls and cook from frozen).

PITA

MAKES: 12

ACTIVE TIME: 30 MINUTES   TOTAL TIME: 1 HOUR 30 MINUTES TO 2 HOURS 30 MINUTES (DEPENDING ON RISING TIME)

2 cups/250g bread flour, plus extra for dusting

1 package (2¼ teaspoons/7g) fast-acting instant yeast

1 teaspoon salt

¼ cup/60ml vegetable oil

½ cup plus 2 tablespoons/ 150ml cold water

This is another bread staple in my house. You can always make a meal quicker by buying these, but they're so amazing when they're baked fresh. Use with Harissa Bean Pizza (p. 22), Paneer Pita (p. 104), and Chicken Shawarma (p. 177).

Place the flour in a large bowl. Add the yeast to one side and salt and oil to the other. Give it all a rough mix with your hands.

Make a well in the center and add the water. Gradually bring the dough together.

Rub the work surface with a little oil and tip the dough out. Knead the dough for about 10 minutes, till it's smooth, shiny, and very stretchy.

Let rise in a bowl, covered with plastic wrap or a tea towel, in a warm place for 1 hour, or until the dough has doubled in size.

Preheat the oven to 480°F/250°C, or the highest temperature you can get it.

Place a baking sheet in the oven.

Tip the dough onto a very lightly dusted surface. Knock out all the air and divide the mixture into 12 equal-size balls. Roll out each ball into an oval shape, about ⅛ inch/3mm thin.

You will need to cook these in batches. Place as many as you can fit on the sheet and bake for 2 to 3 minutes, until they are golden brown and puffed up. Repeat with the remaining dough, keeping the baked pitas wrapped in tea towels to keep warm.

WHITE BUNS

MAKES: 8   TOTAL TIME: 2 HOURS

4 cups/500g bread flour, plus extra for dusting

1 package (2¼ teaspoons/7g) fast-acting instant yeast

2 teaspoons sugar

1 teaspoon salt

1¼ cups/300ml warm water

5 tablespoons/75ml vegetable oil

1 egg, beaten, for glazing

1 teaspoon poppy seeds

I find it's great to have a reliable recipe for lovely soft white rolls that you can keep returning to again and again. I use these for my Fish Pie Burgers (p. 114) but you can, of course, use them for the Corned Beef Subs (p. 108), Falafel (p. 100), Coronation Tuna (p. 96), alongside a soup (p. 130), and absolutely anything else you can think of…

Put the flour into a bowl with the yeast and sugar on one side and the salt on the other. Give them a quick mix, then make a well in the center. Pour in the water and oil and bring everything together gently until it forms a dough. Tip it out onto a floured work surface and knead until the mixture is elastic and smooth. It will be sticky, but be sure not to add any flour to the work surface.

Place back in the bowl, cover with plastic wrap, and let rise in a warm place to double in size (approx. 1 to 1½ hours).

Take the dough out of its bowl and put it on a lightly floured work surface. Have a baking sheet at the ready, lined with parchment paper. Knock the air out of the dough and divide into 8 equal balls. Place them on the sheet about 1 inch/2.5cm apart, cover with a piece of greased plastic wrap, and let rise to double in size again.

Preheat the oven to 450°F/240°C. Brush the rolls with the beaten egg and sprinkle with poppy seeds. Place in the oven and bake for 10 to 15 minutes.

Remove from the oven and wrap in a clean tea towel to help absorb any extra moisture as they cool.

HOMEMADE BUTTER

MAKES: APPROX. 9 OZ BLOCK   **TOTAL TIME:** 30 MINS

2½ cups heavy cream

1 tablespoon sea salt

Put the cream into a mixer, or use a handheld mixer, and whisk on high for about 5 minutes, scraping the sides of the bowl every now and then, until it gets to the soft-peak stage. After that it will quickly get to stiff peaks and then it will curdle. This is exactly what you want. As soon as it does that, it will change fast—you will be able to hear it. There will be a lot of sloshing, where the water separates from the fat. What you should be left with is crumbly-looking butter and liquid in the bottom of the bowl.

Have ready a colander lined with cheesecloth or a thin piece of cotton (e.g., a clean tea towel). Tip the butter into the colander and place it in the sink for all that excess liquid to drain off. As the dripping slows down, give the butter a good squeeze to get rid of as much moisture as possible. Pop into a clean bowl, add the salt, and mix well until the crystals are dispersed. Now either store in a jar or mold into a block and wrap in parchment paper. Refrigerate until needed.

You can customize this however you like. Some sweet options I like are brown sugar butter, apple butter (simply add applesauce), cinnamon butter, vanilla butter, and strawberry butter (add freeze-dried strawberries).

PEANUT BUTTER

MAKES: A 100G JAR   **TOTAL TIME:** 5 MINUTES

3½ cups peanuts

1 teaspoon salt (omit if using salted peanuts)

1 tablespoon honey

4 to 5 tablespoons vegetable oil

You'll need peanut butter for my sheetpan pancake (see p. 24) and the One-Pan Peanut Chicken (see p. 147), but frankly who doesn't need a jar of peanut butter in their cupboard? And it's so much more satisfying when you've made it yourself. You can, of course, swap in practically any nut you want—almonds and cashews work well, too.

Put the nuts in a food processor with the salt, if using, and honey and blitz till the whole thing starts to change texture and becomes a fine paste. Add the oil slowly and watch as it turns to butter in front of your very eyes. As soon as it's smooth and shiny, stop and transfer the mixture to a jar.

GRANOLA

MAKES: APPROX. 17 SERVINGS   **ACTIVE TIME:** 10 MINUTES   **TOTAL TIME:** 45 MINUTES

3 tablespoons melted coconut oil

½ cup plus 1 tablespoon/ 140ml maple syrup or honey

1 teaspoon vanilla bean paste

1 teaspoon almond extract

3⅓ cups/300g rolled oats

⅔ cup/100g sunflower seeds

1 cup/100g sliced almonds

⅔ cup/100g dried cranberries/blueberries/ raisins—or a mix if you prefer

Homemade breakfast, all ready to go in the morning. Serve with yogurt and fresh berries, or with just a dash of milk. Add some chocolate chunks to it for a real treat. You could also use this in the Pruney Granola Bake (p. 43) or the Breakfast Trifle (p. 47).

Preheat the oven to 300°F/150°C and have a lined rimmed baking sheet at the ready. Put the coconut oil, maple syrup, vanilla, and almond extract into a bowl and mix together. Add the oats, sunflower seeds, and almonds and mix really well until everything is coated and looking glossy, then spread the mixture out onto the baking sheet. Bake for 15 minutes. Remove from the oven and scatter the dried fruit over the oats, then bake again for 15 to 20 minutes, or until the oats are a light golden color.

Once ready, remove the sheet from the oven and allow the granola to cool completely. Once cooled, you may need to break up some of the larger pieces, but it's nice to keep some small nuggets. Store in an airtight jar—it will last for up to 1 month.

INDEX

A

almonds: granola 247
    ready breakfast flavored
      porridge 39
slow cooker rice 33
    apples: apple palm pies 193
    ready breakfast flavored
      porridge 39
    "tandoori" oven chicken with
      browned butter rice 178
apricots: coconut barfi truffles 189
    Florentine cookies 189
arancini balls: sweet 209
asparagus: one-pot tortellini 97
avocados: avocado pesto 27–9
    black pepper poke salmon bowls 116

B

bacon: bacon & bean potato skins 92
tatty cakes 49
baked beans: bacon & bean potato
    skins 92
    baked bean falafel 100
    harissa bean pizza 22
bananas: banana tarte tatin with malai
    ice cream 217
    banoffee waffles 56
    burnt butterscotch bananas with
      ice cream and rice pudding 223
bao buns with spicy tuna 160
beans: bacon & bean potato skins 92
    baked bean falafel 100
    harissa bean pizza 22
    lava fries 151
beef: beef and kimchi noodles 81
    lava fries 151
    meatloaf roll 66
    shortcut beef pasties 150
beet: blender beets 71
Bengali bangers and hash smash 134
Bengali spice mix (panch phoran) 237
black and white sandwich cookies 225
black pepper cake 215
black pepper poke salmon bowls 116
Bombay mix potato skins 92

bread: bao buns with spicy tuna 160
    cheese on toast with avocado
      pesto 29
    corned beef sub 108
    egg rolls 60
    English muffin bake 62
    freezing 13
    fried bread with raspberry honey 52
    garlic bread 242
    harissa bean pizza 22
    hoop fish bake 138
    jackfruit curry with no-yeast naan 162
    meatloaf roll 66
    olive and rosemary crown 54
    paneer pita 104
    pecan brie brûlée 84
    pita 243
    pizza parathas 120
    savory French toast 99
    scrap soup 77
    spotted dick bread with homemade
      butter 57
    Thai red pepper soup 130
    ting momos with soy cabbage 171–3
    white buns 244
breakfast trifle 47
brie: pecan brie brûlée 84
brioche: breakfast trifle 47
broccoli: chicken shawarma 177
    hoop fish bake 138
    one-pan peanut chicken 147
burgers: fish pie burgers 114–15
    mushroom mozzarella burgers 133
butter: cod roe pâté 132
    freezing 12
    homemade butter 246
    spotted dick bread with homemade
      butter 57
buttermilk: pruney granola bake 43
    spotted dick bread with homemade
      butter 57
butternut squash: hasselback squash
    with burned garlic rice 180
butterscotch: burnt butterscotch
    bananas with ice cream and rice
      pudding 223

C

cabbage: coleslaw 100
    ting momos with soy cabbage 171–3
cabbage, pickled: black pepper poke
    salmon bowls 116
    edamame wild rice salad 89
cakes & bakes: black pepper cake 215
    choc lime roulade 196–8
    chocolate and orange blossom
      baklava 220
    London cheesecake 205
    peanut butter and jelly sheetpan
      pancake 24
    preserved lemon sheet cake 212
    princess torte cake 226
    pruney granola bake 43
    ras malai cake 232
    speculoos cookie
      sheet cake 218
capers: creamy marinara chicken 86
carrots: black pepper poke salmon
    bowls 116
    coleslaw 100
    corned beef Bombay pie 118
    masala porridge 38
cauliflower hash and eggs 34–5
cereal milk ice cream 224
cheese: bacon & bean potato skins 92
    Bengali bangers and hash smash 134
    blender beets 71
    Bombay mix potato skins 92
    cheese on toast with avocado
      pesto 29
    chili potato skins 92
    corned beef sub 108
    cottage cheese and onion potato
      skins 90
    crustless spinach quiche 83
    English muffin bake 62
    fish stick enchiladas 143
    freezing 12
    kiwi salad 88
    lava fries 151
    macaroni and cheese 62
    mushroom mozzarella burgers 133
    nachos with avocado pesto 29

olive and rosemary crown 54
paneer koftas with vermicelli rice
    165–6
paneer pasta salad 105
paneer pita 104
Parmesan scones with salmon
    paste 64
pecan brie brûlée 84
pesto potato skins 92
pizza parathas 120
poutine 142
sausage and egg sliders 58
savory French toast 99
slow cooker mushroom lasagne 156
sweet potato and goat cheese
    curry 111
sweet potato and goat cheese
    soup 111
sweet potato and goat cheese
    tart 110–11
three cheese crispy pancakes 72
tzatziki quesadillas 73
cheesecake: raspberry cheesecake
    croissants 18
cherries: ready breakfast flavored
    porridge 39
chia seeds: breakfast trifle 47
chia and yogurt ice pops 47
chicken: chicken and pea
    noodles 81
chicken shawarma 177
chicken skewers 106
chicken soup 135
creamy marinara chicken 86
grandmama's curry 158
honey mustard chow mein 106
marinated chicken wings 116
one-pan peanut chicken 147
pecan chili chicken with rice 84
roast chicken with lemon
    couscous 135
"tandoori" oven chicken with
    browned butter rice 178
tzatziki quesadillas 73
chickpeas: creamy marinara chicken 86
paneer koftas with vermicelli rice
    165–6
chili con carne: potato skins 92
chiles: bao buns with spicy tuna 160
blender beets 71

freezing 13
grandmama's curry paste 158
hoop fish bake 138
lava fries 151
nachos with avocado pesto 29
teriyaki salmon with mango salsa 128
three cheese crispy pancakes 72
tzatziki quesadillas 73
chocolate: banoffee waffles 56
choc bar puffs 190
choc chip pan cookie 210
choc lime roulade 196–8
choco momos with raspberry
    sauce 230
chocolate hazelnut mousse 187
chocolate and orange blossom
    baklava 220
chocolate rose panna cotta tart 225
frying pan s'mores 188
gingerbread melt-in-the-middles
    204
ripple éclair pops 214
speculoos cookie sheet cake 218
truffles 198
chorizo fish stew with garlic bread 168
chow mein, honey mustard 106
citrus pudding 195
cloud bread with creamy mackerel
    topping 109
cocoa pikelets with whipped maple
    butter 63
coconut barfi truffles 189
coconut, dried shredded: coconut
    barfi truffles 189
Florentine cookies 109
grandmama's curry 158
London cheesecake 205
ready breakfast flavored
    porridge 39
coconut milk: sticky coconut rice with
    tempered pineapple 30
Thai red pepper soup 130
cod roe pâté 132
coffee: burnt butterscotch frappé 223
pecan rounds with coffee cream 211
coleslaw 100
corned beef: corned beef Bombay
    pie 118
corned beef sub 108
coronation tuna 96

cottage cheese: cottage cheese and
    onion potato skins 90
edamame wild rice salad 89
couscous: creamy marinara chicken 86
roast chicken with lemon
    couscous 135
cream: banana tarte tatin with malai
    ice cream 217
burnt butterscotch bananas with
    ice cream and rice pudding 223
chocolate hazelnut mousse 187
chocolate and orange blossom
    baklava 220
chocolate rose panna cotta tart 225
cod roe pâté 132
creamy mackerel tart 109
homemade butter 246
pecan chili chicken with rice 84
pecan rounds with coffee cream 211
ripple éclair pops 214
saffron rose shrikand 194
slow cooker rice 33
speculoos cookie sheet cake 218
spotted dick bread with homemade
    butter 57
sweet arancini balls 209
sweet risotto 208
cream cheese: choc lime roulade
    196–8
cloud bread with creamy mackerel
    topping 109
fish stick enchiladas 143
pizza parathas 120
crème fraîche: sweet potato and
    goat cheese tart 110–11
croissants: raspberry cheesecake 18
crustless spinach quiche 83
cucumber: kiwi salad 88
tzatziki quesadillas 73
currants: spotted dick bread with
    homemade butter 57
curry: grandmama's curry 158
jackfruit curry with no-yeast naan 162
lamb dansak 148
sweet potato and goat cheese
    curry 111
curry paste: grandmama's curry
    paste 158, 159
my favorite curry paste 240
Thai green curry paste 238

D

dried fruit: apple palm pies 193
   coconut barfi truffles 189
   Florentine cookies 189
   granola 247
   ready breakfast flavored
      porridge 39
   spotted dick bread with
      homemade butter 57
dry spice 237

E

éclairs: ripple éclair pops 214
edamame wild rice salad 89
eggplants: Asian eggplant
      wedges 85
   stir-fried noodles with eggplants 85
eggs: cauliflower hash and
      eggs 34–5
   cloud bread with creamy mackerel
      topping 109
   crustless spinach quiche 83
   egg noodles 81
   egg rolls 60
   fish pie burgers 114–15
   freezing 13
   grapefruit tiramisu 207
   harissa bean pizza 22
   meatloaf roll 66
   pancake batter 241
   prawn Malay rice 95
   saucy citrus pudding 195
   sausage and egg sliders 58
   savory French toast 99
   strawberry milkshake funnel
      cake 200
   sweet potato and goat cheese tart
      110–11
   tatty cakes 49
   three cheese crispy pancakes 72
   watercress quinoa kedgeree 119
English muffin bake 62

F

falafels: baked bean 100
feta cheese: blender beets 71
   kiwi salad 88
   pesto potato skins 92

fish: bao buns with spicy tuna 160
   black pepper poke salmon bowls 116
   chorizo fish stew with garlic bread 168
   cloud bread with creamy mackerel
      topping 109
   coronation tuna 96
   creamy mackerel tart 109
   fish stick enchiladas 143
   fish pie burgers 114–15
   hoop fish bake 138
   marmalade haddock 144
   Parmesan scones with salmon
      paste 64
   teriyaki salmon with mango salsa
   128
   watercress quinoa kedgeree 119
Florentine cookies 189
freezer use 7, 8, 10, 11–15
French toast: savory 99
fruit: breakfast trifle 47
frying pan s'mores 188

G

garlic: garlic bread 168, 242
   grandmama's curry paste 158
   hasselback squash with burned
      garlic rice 180
   my favorite curry paste 240
   Thai green curry paste 238
ginger: bao buns with spicy tuna 160
   edamame wild rice salad 89
   gingerbread melt-in-the-middles 204
   grandmama's curry paste 158
   honey mustard chow mein 106
   jackfruit curry with no-yeast naan 162
   my favorite curry paste 240
   paneer koftas with vermicelli rice
      165–6
   Thai green curry paste 238
gnocchi: one-pan peanut chicken 147
granola 247
grapefruit tiramisu 207

H

haddock: marmalade haddock 144
ham: savory French toast 99
harissa: harissa bean pizza 22
hash browns: Bengali bangers and
   hash smash 134

hasselback squash with burned garlic
   rice 180
hazelnuts: banana tarte tatin with
   malai ice cream 217
   chocolate hazelnut mousse 187
   ready breakfast flavored
      porridge 39
   ripple éclair pops 214
herbs: freezing 13
honey: bao buns with spicy tuna 160
   breakfast trifle 47
   chocolate and orange blossom
      baklava 220
   edamame wild rice salad 89
   fried bread with raspberry
      honey 52
   granola 247
honey mustard chow mein 106
kiwi salad 88
   my favorite curry paste 240
   teriyaki salmon with mango
      salsa 128
hoop fish bake 138
hummus: creamy marinara
   chicken 86

I

ice cream: banana tarte tatin with
   malai ice cream 217
   burnt butterscotch bananas with
      ice cream and rice pudding 223
   cereal milk 224
   shrikand 194

J

jackfruit curry with no-yeast
   naan 162
jam: London cheesecake 205
   peanut butter and jelly sheetpan
      pancake 24
   princess torte cake 226

K

kidney beans: lamb dansak 148
   lava fries 151
kimchi: beef and kimchi noodles 81
kiwi salad 88

L

lamb: butterflied lamb leg with a
    rhubarb and rosemary glaze 154–5
  lamb dansak 148
lava fries 151
leftovers 8, 10
lemons: avocado pesto 27–9
  black pepper poke salmon bowls 116
  fish pie burgers 114–15
  my favorite curry paste 240
  preserved lemon sheet cake 212
  roast chicken with lemon
    couscous 135
  saucy citrus pudding 195
  sweet potato and goat cheese tart
    110–11
lentil and orange soup 76
limes: chili-pecan chicken with rice 84
  choc lime roulade 196–8
  grandmama's curry 158
  honey mustard chow mein 106
  one-pan peanut chicken 147
  princess torte cake 226
  saucy citrus pudding 195
  teriyaki salmon with mango salsa 128
London cheesecake 205

M

macaroni and cheese 62
mackerel: cloud bread with creamy
    mackerel topping 109
  creamy mackerel tart 109
mango: mango and peach mint
    sorbet 184
  mango and peach sorbet float 184
  ready breakfast flavored porridge 39
  teriyaki salmon with mango salsa 128
maple syrup: cocoa pikelets with
    whipped maple butter 63
  granola 247
  paneer koftas with vermicelli rice
    165–6
marinara chicken 86
marmalade haddock 144
marshmallows: frying pan s'mores 188
marzipan: princess torte cake 226
masala porridge 38
mascarpone: grapefruit tiramisu 207
  slow cooker mushroom lasagne 156

three cheese crispy pancakes 72
mayonnaise: baked bean falafel 100
  Bengali bangers and hash smash 134
  black pepper poke salmon bowls 116
  coronation tuna 96
  fish pie burgers 114–15
meatloaf roll 66
microwave ovens 8
milk: burnt butterscotch frappé 223
  chocolate hazelnut mousse 187
  chocolate rose panna cotta tart 225
  cocoa pikelets with whipped maple
    butter 63
  creamy raspberry overnight oats 19
  crustless spinach quiche 83
  English muffin bake 62
  freezing 12
  jackfruit curry with no-yeast naan 162
  pancake batter 241
  princess torte cake 226
  ras malai cake 232
  saucy citrus pudding 195
  slow cooker mushroom lasagne 156
  slow cooker rice 33
  strawberry milkshake funnel cake 200
  sweet arancini balls 209
  sweet risotto 208
muffins: English muffin bake 62
mushrooms: egg rolls 60
  mushroom mozzarella burgers 133
  poutine 142
  sausage and mushroom toad-in-
    the-hole 51
  slow cooker mushroom lasagne 156
  soy mushroom noodles 81
mustard: chicken shawarma 177
  honey mustard chow mein 106
  Parmesan scones with salmon
    paste 64

N

nachos with avocado pesto 29
noodles: honey mustard chow mein 106
  instant noodles 78, 81
  stir-fried noodles with eggplants 85
nutritional yeast: English muffin
    bake 62
  meatloaf roll 66
  poutine 142

nuts: apple palm pies 193
  avocado pesto 27–9
  banana tarte tatin with malai
    ice cream 217
  black pepper poke salmon bowls 116
  chili-pecan chicken with rice 84
  chocolate hazelnut mousse 187
  choco momos with raspberry
    sauce 230
  coconut barfi truffles 189
  Florentine cookies 189
  granola 247
  honey mustard chow mein 106
  one-pan peanut chicken 147
  peanut butter 246
  pecan brie brûlée 84
  pecan rounds with coffee cream 211
  ready breakfast flavored
    porridge 39
  ripple éclair pops 214
  slow cooker rice 33

O

oats: creamy raspberry overnight oats 19
  granola 247
  masala porridge 38
  pruney granola bake 43
  ready breakfast flavored
    porridge 39
olives: egg rolls 60
onions: cod roe pâté 132
  coleslaw 100
  corned beef Bombay pie 118
  corned beef şuh 108
  cottage cheese and onion potato
    skins 90
  fish stick enchiladas 143
  freezing 12
  honey mustard chow mein 106
  kiwi salad 88
  lamb dansak 148
  lava fries 151
  my favorite curry paste 240
  one-tray peanut chicken 147
  paneer pita 104
  poutine 142
  prawn Malay rice 95
  roast chicken with lemon
    couscous 135

sweet potato and goat cheese curry 111

sweet potato and goat cheese tart 110–11

"tandoori" oven chicken with browned butter rice 178

Thai green curry paste 238

ting momos with soy cabbage 171–3

oranges: breakfast trifle 47

chocolate and orange blossom baklava 220

coconut barfi truffles 189

Florentine cookies 189

lentil and orange soup 76

saucy citrus pudding 195

P

pancakes: pancake batter 241

peanut butter and jelly sheetpan pancake 24

three cheese crispy 72

panch phoran 237

paneer: paneer koftas with vermicelll rice 165–6

paneer pasta salad 105

paneer pita 104

Parmesan scones with salmon paste 64

parsnips: shortcut beef pasties 150

passata: creamy marinara chicken 86

fish stick enchiladas 143

pasta: blender beets 71

hoop fish bake 138

macaroni and cheese 62

one-pot tortellini 97

paneer koftas with vermicelli rice 165–6

paneer pasta salad 105

pasta and avocado pesto 29

slow cooker mushroom lasagne 156

pâte: cod roe 132

peaches: mango and peach mint sorbet 184

peanut butter: one-pan peanut chicken 147

peanut butter and jelly sheetpan pancake 24

peanuts: black pepper poke salmon bowls 116

honey mustard chow mein 106

one-pan peanut chicken 147

peanut butter 246

peas: chicken and pea noodles 81

fish pie burgers 114–15

one-pot tortellini 97

piri drumsticks, fries and pea mash 140

prawn Malay rice 95

pecans: chili-pecan chicken with rice 84

pecan brie brûlée 84

pecan rounds with coffee cream 211

peppers: corned beef Bombay pie 118

corned beef sub 108

paneer pita 104

Thai red pepper soup 130

ting momos with soy cabbage 171–3

pesto: potato skins 92

pies & tarts: apple palm pies 193

banana tarte tatin with malai ice cream 217

chocolate 190

chocolate rose panna cotta tart 225

corned beef Bombay pie 118

creamy mackerel tart 109

meatloaf roll 66

shortcut beef pasties 150

sweet potato and goat cheese tart 110–11

pikelets: cocoa flavored with whipped maple butter 63

pineapple: sticky coconut rice with tempered pineapple 30

pine nuts: sweet potato and goat cheese tart 110–11

piri drumsticks, fries and pea mash 140

pistachios: coconut barfi truffles 189

Florentine cookies 189

pita 243

pizza: harissa bean 22

pizza parathas 120

potatoes: Bengali bangers and hash smash 134

chicken soup 135

corned beef Bombay pie 118

corned beef sub 108

cottage cheese and onion potato skins 90

fish pie burgers 114–15

lava fries 151

marmalade haddock 144

piri drumsticks, fries and pea mash 140

potato skins five ways 92

poutine 142

shortcut beef pasties 150

tatty cakes 49

poutine 142

prawn Malay rice 95

preserved lemon sheet cake 212

princess torte cake 226

prunes: pruney granola bake 43

Q

quesadillas: tzatziki 73

quiche: crustless spinach 83

quinoa: watercress quinoa kedgeree 119

tatty cakes 49

R

ras malai cake 232

raspberries: choco momos with raspberry sauce 230

creamy raspberry overnight oats 19

fried bread with raspberry honey 52

raspberry cheesecake croissants 18

ripple éclair pops 214

rhubarb: butterflied lamb leg with a rhubarb and rosemary glaze 154–5

rice: black pepper poke salmon bowls 116

burnt butterscotch bananas with ice cream and rice pudding 223

chili-pecan chicken with rice 84

edamame wild rice salad 89

hasselback squash with burned garlic rice 180

paneer koftas with vermicelli rice 165–6

prawn Malay rice 95

slow cooker rice 33

sticky coconut rice with tempered pineapple 30

sweet arancini balls 209

sweet risotto 208

"tandoori" oven chicken with browned butter rice 178

teriyaki salmon with mango salsa 128
ricotta: creamy raspberry overnight
    oats 19
raspberry cheesecake croissants 18
ripple éclair pops 214

S

saffron rose shrikand 194
salads: edamame wild rice salad 89
    kiwi salad 88
    paneer pasta salad 105
    red onion apple salad 178
salmon: black pepper poke salmon
    bowls 116
    Parmesan scones with salmon
        paste 64
    teriyaki salmon with mango salsa 128
sausages: Bengali bangers and hash
    smash 134
    meatloaf roll 66
    sausage and egg sliders 58
    sausage and mushroom toad-in-
        the-hole 51
scones: Parmesan, with salmon
    paste 64
shrikand ice cream 194
smoked trout: watercress quinoa
    kedgeree 119
s'mores, frying pan 188
snow peas: grandmama's curry 158
sorbet: mango and peach mint 184
soup: chicken soup 135
    lentil and orange soup 76
    one-pot tortellini 97
    spicy scrap soup 77
    sweet potato and goat cheese
        soup 111
    Thai red pepper soup 130
sour cream: chili potato skins 92
    lava fries 151
    nachos with avocado pesto 29
soy mushroom noodles 81
spaghetti hoops: hoop fish bake 138
speculoos cookie sheet cake 218
spice mixes 237
spicy scrap soup 77
spinach: avocado pesto 27–9
    crustless spinach quiche 83
    harissa bean pizza 22

soy mushroom noodles 81
spotted dick bread with homemade
    butter 57
squash: hasselback squash with
    burned garlic rice 180
stir-fries: honey mustard chow
    mein 106
    stir-fried noodles with eggplants 85
strawberry milkshake funnel cake 200
sweet potatoes: sweet potato and
    goat cheese curry 111
    sweet potato and goat cheese
        soup 111
    sweet potato and goat cheese
        tart 110–11
sweet risotto 208
sweet corn: fish stick enchiladas 143
    grandmama's curry 158

T

tahini: kiwi salad 88
"tandoori" oven chicken with
    browned butter rice 178
tandoori spice mix 238
tapenade: olive and rosemary
    crown 54
tarts see pies & tarts
tatty cakes 49
teriyaki salmon with mango
    salsa 128
textured vegetable protein: ting
    momos with soy cabbage 171–3
Thai green curry paste 238
Thai red pepper soup 130
ting momos with soy cabbage 171–3
tiramisu: grapefruit 207
toad-in-the-hole, sausage and
    mushroom 51
tomato soup: lava fries 151
tomatoes: chorizo fish stew with garlic
    bread 168
    English muffin bake 62
    hoop fish bake 138
    marmalade haddock 144
    tatty cakes 49
tortillas: egg rolls 60
    fish stick enchiladas 143
    tzatziki quesadillas 73
trifle: breakfast 47

truffles 198
tuna: bao buns with spicy tuna 160
    coronation tuna 96
turkey: savory French toast 99
turkey bacon: tatty cakes 49
tzatziki quesadillas 73

V

vegetables: spicy scrap soup 77
vegetarian bacon: savory French
    toast 99
    tatty cakes 49

W

waffles: banoffee 56
walnuts: avocado pesto 27–9
watercress: paneer pita 104
    sweet potato and goat cheese
        curry 111
    sweet potato and goat cheese tart
        110–11
    watercress quinoa kedgeree 119
white buns 244

Y

yogurt: breakfast trifle 47
    chia and yogurt ice pops 47
    chicken shawarma 177
    mango and peach mint sorbet 184
    masala porridge 38
    paneer koftas with vermicelli rice
        165–6
    Parmesan scones with salmon
        paste 64
    pizza parathas 120
    saffron rose shrikand 194
    "tandoori" oven chicken with
        browned butter rice 178
    tzatziki quesadillas 73
Yorkshire pudding: sausage and
    mushroom toad-in-the-hole 51

Z

zucchini: creamy marinara
    chicken 86

THANKS

Writing recipes is the gift that keeps giving and giving. Just imagine . . . My kitchen, not very big, is functional for family and home, but was never created or designed for the force that is recipe writing. When I am in that world I am engulfed and intoxicated in the most harmless, euphoric way possible. I dart around. It looks aimless but I do know where I'm going (most of the time). Tapping a few keys on my laptop, carefully placed away from any liquids. I make quick notes on my jotting pad. Check the oven. Click the timer, wipe down the surface, clear away the toaster, pour a glass of water, and fill the dishwasher a little more.

I imagine up a new recipe and there in the back of my mind tick tick ticking away is, What shall I make for dinner? Shall I cook dinner? Or shall I just pop a dinner out of the freezer? Or, they could just eat the cake that I'm testing. It's always my last resort, but great for gathering "Who's your favorite parent" points.

But once I am out of my writing, crazy-woman phase, once I have cleared up, once everything is put back into its place, once I have wiped away my greasy fingermarks off the handles of the cupboards and disinfected the kitchen to within an inch of its life, the work continues.

So thank you to all of you who have worked so hard to breathe life into this book.

Thank you to the recipe testers, Emma, Rosie, and Katy, for going through each recipe one by one and for recognizing the recipes I may have written up at midnight, that nobody could understand, not even me! We got there in the end.